Old Dog, New Clicks

Online Industrial and B2B Marketing Know-How for the 21st Century

Bob DeStefano

Gale Media, Inc., Lafayette, CO

Gale Media, Inc.
2569 Park Lane, Suite 200
Lafayette, CO 80026
303-443-5060
www.mdm.com

Gale Media is a market-leading information services and publishing company. Its two business units – Modern Distribution Management and MDM Analytics – provide knowledge products and services to professionals in industrial product and wholesale distribution markets. Since 1967, MDM has been the definitive resource for distribution management best practices, competitive intelligence and market trends through its twice-monthly newsletter, market intelligence reports, books and conferences. MDM Analytics provides proprietary market research and analytic services to profile market share and account potential for industrial products.

Chuck and Beans cartoon courtesy of Hallmark Licensing, LLC.

ISBN 978-0-9906738-3-5

Acknowledgments

To my beautiful daughters Amanda and Rebecca.
You are the light of my life. Always remember – you become what you think about.

To my parents and sister.
Thank you for the endless amount of love and support you always provided.

To the talented team at SVM E-Marketing Solutions.
Thank you for sharing my passion for teaching and helping people succeed.

To Tom, Jenel and the fine folks at Modern Distribution Management.
Thank you for being such wonderful partners, especially on this project.

Contents

Introduction

1999. Many of us look back on that time longingly. In some ways, the world and our lives were much simpler. Terrorism was something that only happened thousands of miles away in countries most people couldn't find on a map. We were in the middle of a soaring stock market thanks to the dot-com boom. Real estate values were just beginning their astronomic rise. Even marketing was much simpler.

As a distributor or manufacturer in 1999, you could rely on a handful of tried-and-true marketing tactics to grow your business. Face-to-face sales were the heart and soul of your marketing efforts. Pounding the pavement and calling on customers were the tactics most relied on by industrial companies.

This was complemented by an inside sales team waiting for inbound sales calls, often coupled with outbound telemarketing. To help get that phone to ring, some companies leveraged print advertising in trade magazines, industry directories and the Yellow Pages. Some companies added direct mail and trade shows into the mix.

These were the early days of the Internet. As recently as the year 2000, only 50 percent of all U.S. households had home computers with Internet access. More and more websites were springing up, but most B2B business was still done old school. Eventually, some forward-thinking companies began to embrace the new online world by creating a simple website coupled with some email marketing. This marketing mix was all you needed in 1999 to remain competitive.

But then something happened that fundamentally changed how we do business.

Do you remember life before Google?

In the late 1990s, Google came on the scene and quickly evolved from a Stanford research project into the definitive resource for all knowledge and information available on the Internet. Before Google, we had to rely on libraries, volumes of encyclopedias, printed directories, catalogs and other offline resources when we wanted to learn more about anything. Now, the world's resources can be accessed within seconds just by performing a simple search.

Google has fundamentally changed our lives. According to a recent research study performed by Deloitte, 72 percent of us use search engines like Google at least once per day to find information online. Google has become the first stop for many when we are researching products at work, at home or even in a retail setting on our smartphones. From a business perspective, online presence is crucial because it is the most public face of your company and the primary way people connect with you.

How has Google changed your life? Do you use it often to research

Introduction

products and companies before you buy? If you use it so often, don't you think your potential customers do as well? What will they find when your company bubbles up? Will they like what they see and buy from you? If these questions make you uncomfortable, do not fret. This book is designed to help you master the art of industrial marketing in the 21st Century. Maybe we can even help teach an old dog some new clicks!

For generations, distributors and manufacturers relied heavily on face-to-face selling as the primary driver for new business growth. While the role of the salesperson is still critical, your old tactics are no longer enough to compete in this rapidly-evolving marketplace. The changing face – and needs – of your customers combined with the rise of online and mobile technologies in the workplace have rendered your old tactics inadequate. If you're still relying on marketing strategies from the last decade, your company's success may be in question for the next decade. It's time to step up and take action.

You may be thinking: "I've heard all of this before. The Web has been a commercial medium for over 20 years, and I'm still here even though I ignored it." I must assure you that this time it's different. I'll present hard data to make the case as to why now is the time you need to think differently about your current marketing programs, as well as why you need to evolve these programs to succeed in the connected world.

Chapter 1
Why Now is the Time
to Embrace Online Marketing

Yes, distributors and manufacturers have relied for decades on a variety of offline marketing activities to grow their businesses. But regardless of your stance on new techniques and methods, the fact is that traditional marketing activities are declining in relevance and effectiveness. I'm not the one telling you these traditional activities are becoming less effective; you told me! Every two years the National Association of Wholesaler-Distributors produces a report titled *Facing the Forces of Change* in which the NAW surveys wholesalers and distributors to gain insights into key trends impacting the success of its companies. According to a recent publication of this study, in-person sales calls, which distributors rely upon so heavily, will become 18 percent less relevant in the near future; direct print mailings will become 8 percent less relevant; exhibiting at trade shows and in-person events will be 7 percent and 5 percent less relevant, respectively. Telemarketing and print advertising will each only be 1 percent less relevant, but that's probably because they were not very relevant to begin with.

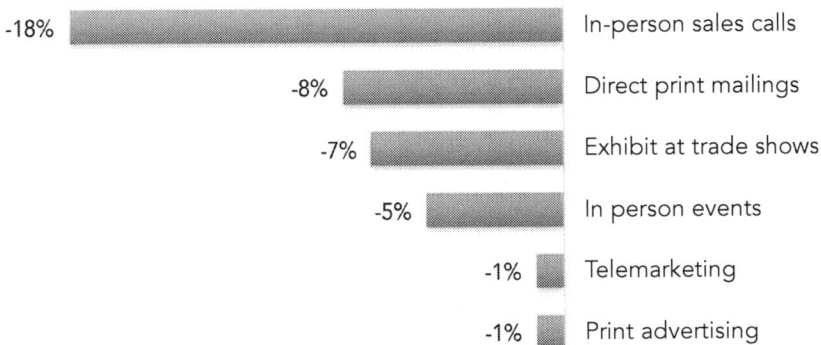

-18%	In-person sales calls
-8%	Direct print mailings
-7%	Exhibit at trade shows
-5%	In person events
-1%	Telemarketing
-1%	Print advertising

Source: NAW *Facing the Forces of Change*

At the same time, survey participants feel that online marketing activities will grow in relevance in the coming years. According to the study, search engine marketing will be 23 percent more relevant and company websites will be 20 percent more relevant. In addition, social network participation will be 18 percent more relevant and email marketing will be 17 percent more relevant. Finally, webinars will be 16 percent more relevant and online advertising will be 6 percent more relevant. Clearly industrial companies are predicting a near-term shift from the offline world to the online world.

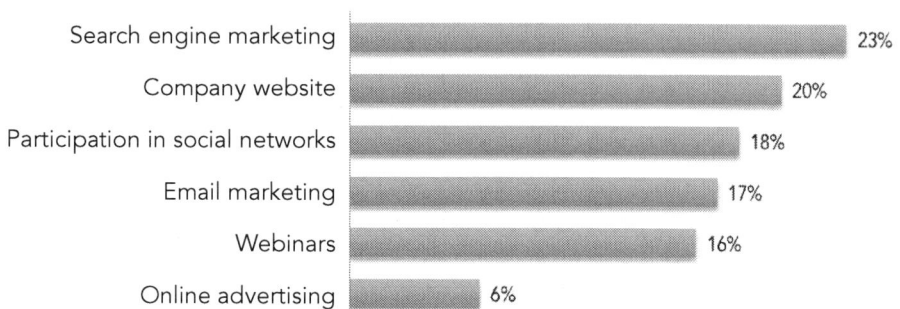

Category	Percentage
Search engine marketing	23%
Company website	20%
Participation in social networks	18%
Email marketing	17%
Webinars	16%
Online advertising	6%

Source: NAW *Facing the Forces of Change*

The changing face of your customer

Why is this dramatic shift from the offline to the online happening? The face of your customer is changing faster than ever in recent history. Many marketers often forget they are selling to people, not companies. Right now you are doing business with three separate and distinct groups of people: baby boomers, Generation Xers and millennials. The workplace is being taken over by the latter two groups, which I like to refer to collectively as "Generation Net." Generation Net has radically different needs, desires and expectations about how business should be conducted. And you need to learn how to meet the needs of this group if you wish to remain competitive in the future.

To highlight the vast differences between these groups, let's spend some time getting to know them. I will begin with the group you are most used to doing business with: the **baby boomers**. Born between 1946 and

1964, there are 75 million in total with 51.2 million baby boomers in the workforce. This group has a unique set of characteristics:

- **Independent:** Baby boomers are confident, independent and self-reliant. They grew up during an era of great reform with the women's rights movement and the civil rights movement; they believed they could change the world. They questioned established authority systems and challenged the status quo their entire lives.

- **Goal-oriented workaholics:** Baby boomers live to work. They are extremely hard-working and motivated by position, perks and prestige. Baby boomers relish long work weeks and define them-selves by their professional accomplishments and the fruits of their labor.

- **Skittish about technology:** Baby boomers are slow adopters of technology. They clearly remember a time when you had to get out of your chair to change the channel on a black-and-white TV. There were only three main channels to choose from, and only one came through clearly if you positioned the antenna just right. Phones weren't smart; they had rotary dials and were connected to a wall in the kitchen confined by a long, curly cord. As computers and online technologies grew in importance, this group cautiously and slowly embraced them. Since they were your primary customers over the past decade, it was easy for you to ignore the online world and still be successful.

The second customer group you are doing business with is **Generation X**. This is my generation. Born between 1965 and 1980, there are 66 million in total with 52.7 million Gen Xers in the workforce. This group's unique characteristics include:

- **Individualistic and resourceful:** Generation X came of age in an era of two-income families, rising divorce rates and a faltering economy. As they grew up, women joined the workforce in large numbers, spawning the age of the "latchkey kid." As a result, Generation X is independent, resourceful and self-reliant.

- **Values work/life balance and versatility:** Where baby boomers "lived to work," Generation Xers "work to live." They appreciate fun in the workplace and have a work hard/play hard mentality. They are hard workers but want to balance that with time with friends and family. Also, having witnessed the mergers, acquisitions and layoffs their parents suffered, Generation Xers resolved early on to take charge of their own destiny. The more degrees and experiences they can acquire, the more they feel they are able to manage opportunity.

- **Tech savvy:** This group grew up during the emergence of many of the technologies we now take for granted. As kids, they played video games at home and in arcades. Cable TV appeared in their homes, offering plenty of entertainment choices. They did homework on personal computers. As they entered the workforce, cell phones, email and the Web became business tools. While their desire to do business with you online has been there for a while, it did not matter to you because Generation X is low in numbers.

This next customer group is the game changer: the **millennials**. Born between 1981 and 1999, there are 75 million in total with 53.5 million already in the workforce. This is the largest adult demographic in the workplace. They already outnumber Generation Xers and baby boomers in the workforce and many millennials are still in high school. As with the two other demographic groups, this group also has a unique set of characteristics:

- **Team-oriented:** Millennials have a pack mentality. As young children, they had group play dates. As they aged, they participated in team sports and went out on group dates, with multiple couples and singles intermingling as friends and equals. They value teamwork and need the ongoing input and affirmation of others. Millennials are also very good at affirming others and highlighting others' accomplishments.

- **Achievement-oriented – and attention-craving:** Millennials were coddled and pampered by their parents. They grew up hearing "good job" for everything they did. When they played team sports, *everybody* got a trophy, no matter what place they came in. As adults, they crave attention in the form of frequent praise and reassurance.

- **Digital natives:** Millennials are hyperconnected technology masters. This group was born with a computer mouse in their hands. They don't know a world without the Internet, cell phones and text messaging. Social networking sites like Facebook were created by millennials for millennials. As new technologies are introduced, millennials are quick to adopt and master them. Millennials demand that you do business with them online – and due to their huge numbers, you'd better take notice and respond.

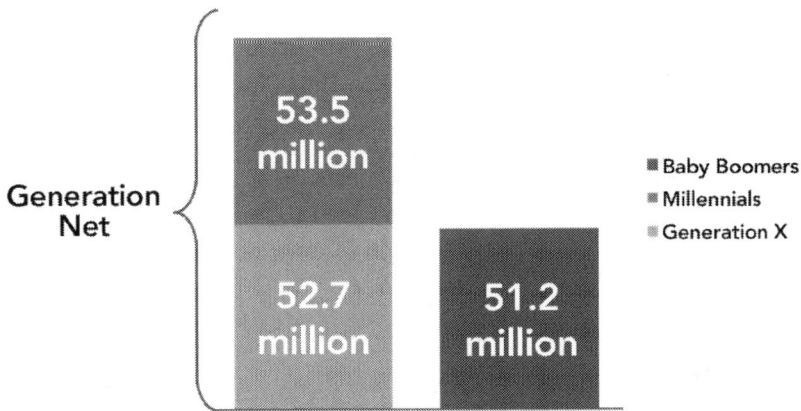

Generation Net

53.5 million

52.7 million

51.2 million

■ Baby Boomers
■ Millennials
■ Generation X

Source: Pew Research Center

It is important for you to address the changing face of your customer now, because we have reached a point where Generation Net (Generation X and the millennials) outnumbers the boomers in the workplace. And this trend is going to continue, because every single day 10,000 baby boomers reach retirement age, while 10,000 millennials turn 21 and enter the workforce. As Generation Net continues to grow in numbers, so will the technology demands they place on your company.

Generation Net is online

It is an understatement to say that Generation Net prefers to work and play online. A number of researchers have studied the differences between the generations over the years. Look at the astounding amount of time Generation Net spends online in the connected world.

Do you own a smartphone?

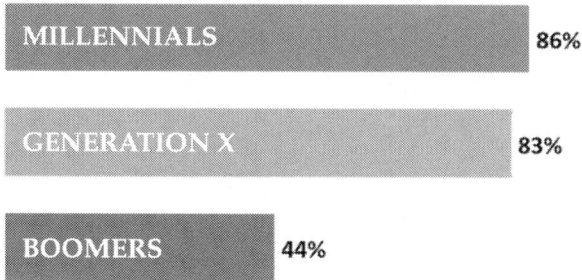

MILLENNIALS 86%

GENERATION X 83%

BOOMERS 44%

Source: Pew Research Center

Generation Net loves their smartphones; 86 percent of millennials and 83 percent of Generation X own an Internet-enabled smartphone with email and mobile apps. In comparison, only 44 percent of baby boomers own a smartphone. Generation Net loves their smartphones so much that many sleep with their phones.

Do you sleep with your mobile phone?

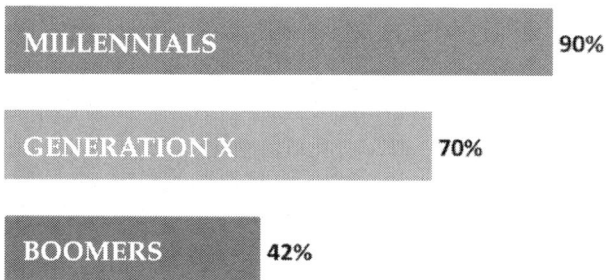

MILLENNIALS 90%

GENERATION X 70%

BOOMERS 42%

Source: Pew Research Center

Why Now is the Time to Embrace Online Marketing

Ninety percent of millennials and 70 percent of Generation X sleep with their mobile phones. At first, I found the idea that 42 percent of boomers sleep with their mobile phones a bit surprising. However, after thinking about this, it makes sense. They are most likely sleeping with their phone because they are waiting for a text or call from their millennial child who is still out for the night!

Do you connect to the Web from your mobile phone?

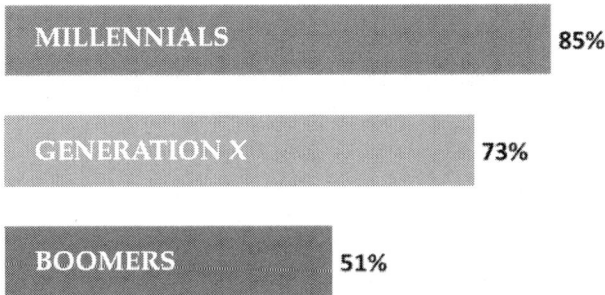

MILLENNIALS	85%
GENERATION X	73%
BOOMERS	51%

Source: Pew Research Center

You cannot assume that Generation Net is accessing your website from a computer on their desk. A full 85 percent of millennials and 73 percent of Generation X access the Web from their mobile phones on the go. If your website is not optimized to display well on the small screen, Generation Net will have difficulty doing business with you online.

Do you use social networking websites?

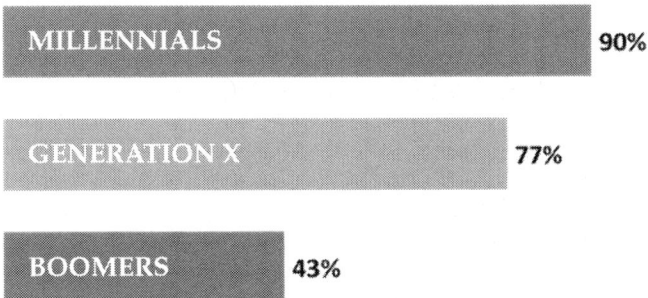

MILLENNIALS	90%
GENERATION X	77%
BOOMERS	43%

Source: Pew Research Center

Generation Net enjoys socializing online; 90 percent of millennials and 77 percent of Generation X use social networking websites. In contrast, less than half of baby boomers use these sites to communicate and share. And I suspect many of those boomers are just checking out what their kids and grandkids are up to. But you can no longer ignore the social media phenomenon. If your company does not become social, it will be a liability as your Generation Net customers grow in prominence.

How many texts do you send and receive per month?

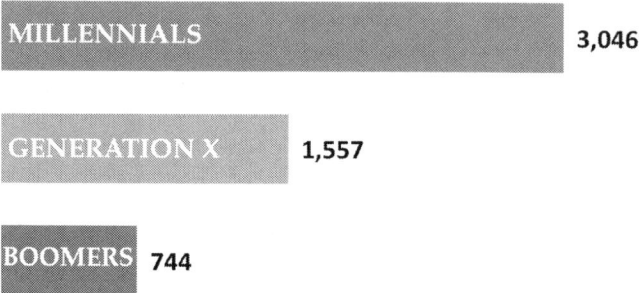

MILLENNIALS	3,046
GENERATION X	1,557
BOOMERS	744

Source: Experian Marketing Services' Simmons

Generation Net prefers quick bursts of information to long conversations. Millennials average more than 3,000 texts per month – almost 100 per day. Generation X texts are about half of that volume at over 1,500. Attention boomer salespeople: Generation Net does not want to talk with you, so don't pick up the phone and call them with a sales pitch. To effectively reach this group, you will have to creatively change your communication behavior.

Do you get most of your news from the Web?

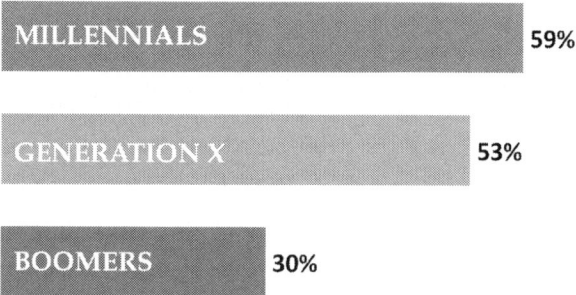

MILLENNIALS	59%
GENERATION X	53%
BOOMERS	30%

Source: Pew Research Center

Fifty-nine percent of millennials and 53 percent of Generation X get most of their news from the Web. If your website is not the best reflection of everything your company has to offer, this group will never know how well you can serve them.

Do you purchase business goods online?

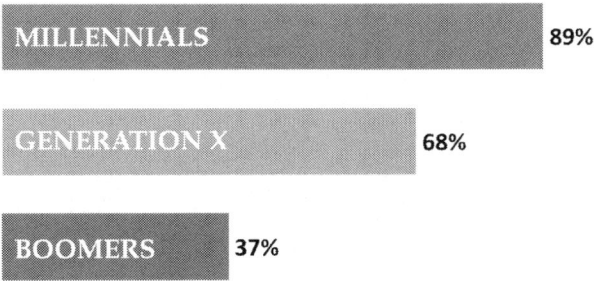

Group	Percent
MILLENNIALS	89%
GENERATION X	68%
BOOMERS	37%

Source: Accenture – B2B Procurement Study

If your company does not have a sound e-commerce strategy, these statistics should have you quaking in your boots: 89 percent of millennials purchase business goods online and 68 percent of Generation X buys business goods online. Even 37 percent of the technology-challenged boomer customers buy business goods on the Web. Your website can no longer exist as a static brochure. Distributors need to sell online, and manufacturers need to sell direct online or partner with distributors that can do it for them.

Generation Net is decimating business models

Generation Net has been growing in prominence over the past 10 years, and the way its population prefers to do business is decimating business models. Their desire for instant access to purchase goods and services online and on the go has killed a number of formerly dominant business models and left many others on life support.

Music retailers: Boomers and early Generation Xers witnessed the evolution of music platforms from vinyl records to 8-tracks and cassettes to digital CDs. Music retailers evolved with the times by restocking their stores with the latest music format. When the millennials and young Gen

Xers became music consumers, they changed the game. They wanted digital access to their entire library of songs on a small portable device, and they wanted to add to this music library instantly online. Apple responded and created the first commercially viable device and online music store with the iPod and iTunes store. As a result, Apple is the largest music retailer in the world, while Tower Records and Sam Goody – remember them? – have vanished.

Video rental shops: When Generation Net wanted to watch a movie at home, they grew tired of driving to the local video rental shop hoping to find one of the five copies of the movie they wished to watch. They wanted instant access to a virtually limitless library of movies and shows that they can watch on their television or mobile device. Broadband cable companies like Comcast and Verizon stepped up to meet this need, as did online media retailers like Apple's iTunes. And of course, we can't forget about Netflix and Amazon. As a result, the formerly dominant video rental company, Blockbuster, declared bankruptcy, was purchased by the Dish Network and has been busy shuttering stores in strip malls throughout the nation.

Book retailers: As with music and movies, Generation Net wanted digital online access to books. Amazon was quick to service this need by creating the Kindle e-book reader and supplying an enormous collection of e-books in its online store. Barnes & Noble shot back with its own creation, the Nook, coupled with e-book titles in its own online storefront. While this was going on, the third largest retailer of books, Borders, sat idly by. They ignored the e-book revolution and were forced into bankruptcy.

Newspaper and magazine publishing: Publishers of newspapers and magazines were quick to embrace the Web in the mid-1990s to serve Generation Net. The problem is they did not give much thought to how it would impact their business model. Traditional print publications largely rely on advertising revenue, so these publishers created online versions of their content and offered it for free, assuming they would make their money from online banner advertisements. They eventually learned that banner ads don't pay as well, and, with online access to their content, fewer people purchased their print publication. Many of the iconic print publishers like the Tribune Company and the Journal Register Company declared bankruptcy, and many jobs were lost to keep the remaining publications afloat. It will be interesting to see how Jeff Bezos from Amazon will impact newspaper publishing with his purchase of *The Washington Post*.

Camera film: When was the last time you held a roll of film? Generation Net wanted nothing to do with it. They would be horrified by the idea of being limited to 24 or 36 pictures and not seeing the creative output until it was developed hours or days later by the local Fotomat. Generation Net wants to take unlimited pictures anywhere from their smartphone. They want to view and edit them instantly and share them with 1,463 of their "friends" on Facebook or, increasingly, Instagram. As a result, the American institution known as Kodak declared bankruptcy in 2012 and is trying to re-emerge as a corporate imaging company.

Big-box electronics retailers: I believe big-box electronics retailers, such as Best Buy, will be next in line to be radically changed by Generation Net. A concept known as showrooming is threatening their business model. Generation Net engages in showrooming when they drive to Best Buy to touch and test a new flat screen TV but buy it on the Web from an online retailer with a lower price. Attention distributors: If you have retail locations where customers come to shop, you may already be a victim of showrooming. Compare your prices to the online competition to see where you stand.

Generation Net is coming after your business model, as well. In some industries, online legends like Amazon are already going after your customers with offerings like Amazon Business. It's time to get serious about online marketing.

The growth of online and mobile has only just begun

If you think the world is online now, you ain't seen nothing yet. The growth of online and mobile has just begun. According to a study performed by Cisco Systems,[1] global Internet traffic has increased more than fivefold over the past years and will increase nearly threefold by 2019. More than 3.9 billion people (more than 51 percent of the world's population) will be online. Even in remote locations without electricity and running water, people will be going online with smartphones powered by solar chargers. If your online marketing strategy has been nonexistent thus far, this represents a great opportunity for you to claim your piece of the pie.

The importance of mobile is also growing by leaps and bounds. According to the comScore Digital Future in Focus study,[2] in early 2014 mobile devices, like smartphones and tablets, began outpacing traditional computers as the primary way that people access information online in their personal lives and their business lives. Therefore, you need to embrace mobile marketing, in addition to online marketing, if you want to be successful in selling to Generation Net.

---

1   Cisco Visual Networking Index, http://www.cisco.com/c/en/us/solutions/service-provider/visual-networking-index-vni/index.html

2   Lella, Adam, and Andrew Lipsman, "2015 U.S. Digital Future in Focus," comScore, March 26, 2015, https://www.comscore.com/Insights/Presentations-and-Whitepapers/2015/2015-US-Digital-Future-in-Focus.

Chapter 2
The 21st Century Marketing Road Map

Now you know why NOW is the time to get off the sidelines and embrace online marketing. But the problem for most manufacturers and distributors is that they don't know where to start. To many, online marketing is a big black box of mystery. My job is to lift that cloud of mystery and show you that box is actually a toolbox you can put to work to produce results for your company. To help you put your online marketing toolbox to work, I have defined the 21st Century Marketing Road Map: nine ideas to leverage online marketing to produce bottom-line results.

- **Don't fall for marketing misnomers.** Let's debunk some common myths about marketing to ensure you begin this journey with the right mindset. Marketing is vital to your organization's success. However, to be successful, you need to think of marketing not as another expense, but as a measurable investment that will attract customers to you when they are ready to do business.

- **You Have an Online Brand (Whether You Like It or Not).** Make no mistake – people are Googling your company and what they find represents your online brand. You simply can't ignore your company's online image. If you build a solid online brand, you can influence and shape how your customers see your company, which will result in more people wanting to do business with you.

- **Become a content marketer.** According to a survey by Roper Public Affairs,[1] 80 percent of business decision-makers prefer to get information

---

1 Devaney, Tim, and Tom Stein, "Use Content Marketing to Boost Your Business," Forbes, Jan. 23, 2013, http://www.forbes.com/sites/capitalonespark/2013/01/23/tell-dont-sell-use-content-marketing-to-boost-your-business/#2e006696615c76120fc2615c.

from articles, not advertisements. In marketing, content is king. You need to stop marketing your products and start marketing your knowledge. Transform your company into the go-to resource for business-building ideas.

■ **Make your website the hub of your marketing.** Your website is the most public face of your company. More people will see your website than will visit your location, read your literature or speak with your salespeople. Make the most of this powerful marketing tool by transforming it into a customer-focused, lead-generation machine.

■ **Help customers find you.** Generation Net wants to find you at the moment they have a product or service need. When that need arises, they turn to search engines like Google or Bing. Search engine marketing offers you a tremendous opportunity to get in front of motivated customers that are actively searching for your products and services.

■ **Nurture relationships with social media.** Social media marketing is the new public relations. However, instead of pitching the media, you are pitching your peers. By sharing useful and relevant content on social networks, your message can achieve tremendous reach as your connections share your content with their connections, who share it with their connections, who share it with their connections, and so on, and so on, and so on.

■ **Nurture relationships with email marketing.** When email is used as a nurturing tool, instead of a prospecting tool, it offers you an opportunity to build an ongoing, interactive dialogue with your customers on a measurable, cost-efficient basis. By sending educational email newsletters, as well as personalized product promotions, you show your customers that you understand them and their needs. This repeatedly reinforces that you value them and builds their trust in your company.

■ **Optimize your marketing for mobile.** Smartphones and tablets are becoming the primary tool for going online. Prepare your company for the mobile revolution by designing your website and online content for the small screen.

- **Make your marketing measurable.** Department store titan John Wanamaker once said: "Half my advertising is wasted, I just don't know which half." Well, Mr. Wanamaker would love 21st century marketing because everything is completely measurable. Forget about relying on gut-feel or subjective measures when judging your marketing activities. Armed with Web and marketing analytics, you will know exactly which activities to cut and which to continue.

The balance of this book will walk you through the 21st Century Marketing Road Map. For each of these concepts, I will provide you with tips, ideas and best practices you can put to work immediately. My goal is to help you transform your company into an online marketing success.

Grab another cup of coffee and let's get started.

Chapter 3
Don't Fall for
Marketing Misnomers

The first step in the 21st Century Marketing Road Map is to begin with the right mindset. Keeping a positive outlook, being resilient and remaining flexible enough to consider new approaches is the basis of any successful marketer's mindset. But through my working with manufacturers and distributors for more than 20 years, I have found that many people have misconceptions about what marketing is and the role it plays in their companies. So, before we dig into strategies and tactics, let's take a look at some of those misconceptions and try to focus on basic truths about marketing.

Marketing is an investment, not an expense

If you think of marketing merely as an expense, chances are you're doing it wrong. Instead, think of marketing as an investment that will produce a measurable return in the form of qualified leads and bankable sales. Just as you would carefully review the return on investment for stocks, bonds and mutual funds in your retirement portfolio, carefully evaluate the return on investment in your company's marketing portfolio.

What type of return on investment should your marketing produce?

First, your marketing should help you attract prospects or new customers. The key to success is targeting your marketing efforts to make sure you are in front of the right people at the right time. Attracting new customers is where most companies spend the majority of their marketing dollars and time. This is unfortunate because it's also the most challenging and expensive result to achieve. It is much easier to sell to existing customers than it is to new ones because you have already earned their trust and you have credibility. Your marketing should also produce re-sults by getting existing customers to:

- Spend more

- Come back more often to buy from you

- Refer new business to you

There are riches in niches

Now that you're thinking of marketing as an investment, let's talk about the best way to deploy that investment. There is a paradox in marketing you need to embrace: The smaller your target market, the bigger your opportunity. This may seem counterintuitive, because you may think marketing your business to the widest possible audience – trying to be all things to all people – is the best way to succeed. Nope! If you say your target customer is "everyone," the reality is you are targeting no one. Or, to put it another way, when you try to be all things to all people, no one will remember you. You need to become a niche marketer.

There are a number of significant benefits of focusing on a niche. First, you have fewer competitors because fewer companies focus on your specialized target market.

Second, you become a specialist, and everyone wants to work with a specialist. You understand your customer's needs more thoroughly, thus your solution becomes more valuable and attractive. Your position in the market becomes stronger, which causes your reputation to spread rapidly throughout your target market. Finally, your marketing is more effective and less expensive. Since you know exactly who your ideal customer is and where to market to reach them, you can spend less time and money getting your message out. You're also less likely to ostracize or offend potential customers by marketing efforts that aren't geared to their specific needs, wants and interests.

How do you identify your ideal niche or target market? There are a num-ber of things to consider when defining your target market, and I recom-mend using a combination of these depending on your business.

- **Industry**: If you market to other businesses, focus your efforts on the specific industries you serve best.

- **Geography**: If you need to physically deliver your products or perform your service in a given geographic area, geography will help define your niche.

- **Job function**: Remember, you are not doing business with companies; you're doing business with people. Therefore, job function or role is part of your niche. Are they the end-users of your product? Are they purchasing agents? Are they business owners who wear multiple hats?

- **Demographics**: What common characteristics do your customers share? Examples of demographic characteristics can include income level, age and gender.

- **Psychographics**: In addition, think about common interests, opinions or personality characteristics the people you are working with share. Examples might include amateur woodworkers, classic car enthusiasts or neat freaks.

How will you know if you identified an ideal niche? An ideal niche market will have the following qualities:

- They have a specialized need or interest.

- Your offering satisfies this specialized need because you specialize in filling that need.

- They have money to spend and are willing to part with it to satisfy this need because they value your offering.

- They are easy to reach, so it's easy to get your message in front of them.

- The niche – or a handful of smaller profitable niches – is large enough to support your business.

Marketing ≠ sales; marketing feeds sales

Too many manufacturers and distributors consider marketing and sales to be synonymous. They feel that if they have a sales force, they also have a marketing force. But this just isn't true. Salespeople are critical for building relationships with customers, as well as closing new business. However, your salespeople should not be responsible for prospecting or for generating leads. That's what marketing is for!

Marketing should feed sales by attracting a steady stream of motivated people who are interested in doing business with you. They should provide a variety of offers and calls to action to get people to reach out and into your sales funnel. Once they're in the sales funnel, your salespeople can do the great job they were born to do: convert happy prospects into happy customers.

Market with a magnet, not a megaphone

Megaphone marketing is SHOUTING AT MANY with the hopes of attracting a few. Successful companies have realized that megaphone marketing tactics just don't work. Examples of megaphone tactics include print advertising, Yellow Page advertising, directory advertising, untargeted banner advertising, cold calls and mass email blasts. Megaphone marketing tactics no longer work because of a fundamental shift in customer behavior. Customers don't want to be interrupted, and megaphone marketing is an interruption. Customers want to be in control of the information they receive; with megaphone marketing, the company is in control.

A more effective and efficient approach is magnet marketing. Magnet marketing helps customers find you at the very moment they have a need for your products and services. It allows you to earn trust by providing customers with information they value, which will attract them to your website to do business. Examples of magnet marketing tactics include content marketing, search engine optimization, pay-per-click advertising and social media marketing. Not only do magnet marketing tactics generate more leads and sales, but they are also less expensive.

According to research from HubSpot,[1] companies that focus on magnet marketing tactics have a 62 percent lower cost per lead than companies that focus on megaphone marketing tactics.

Remember, your Generation Net customers are not only tech-savvy, they're pitch-savvy. Don't try to clobber them over the head with how great your products or prices are or speak so broadly that they can't see themselves benefiting from your offer. The idea is to attract them into a relationship with your company based on mutually beneficial outcomes. To paraphrase an old ad scheme from back in the day: If you want to get their attention, whisper, don't shout. It's better to show them how great you are than to tell them.

1   Miller, Melissa, "Inbound Leads Cost 62% Less than Outbound," HubSpot, Mar. 1, 2011, http://blog.hubspot.com/blog/tabid/6307/bid/10172/Inbound-Leads-Cost-62-Less-than-Outbound-New-Data.aspx

Don't Fall for Marketing Misnomers

Chapter 4

You Have an Online Brand (Whether You Like It or Not)

Most industrial companies give very little thought to branding. They view a brand as something intangible that doesn't have any hard consequences. What is a brand, anyway? Is it a logo? Is it a tagline? Is it an advertising campaign? I think Jeff Bezos, founder of Amazon, put it best when he said, "Your brand is what people say about you when you're not in the room."

In the online world, there is no hiding your brand, and trust me, people are talking.

Why does online image and branding matter?

As we learned earlier, according to a study by Deloitte, more than 70 percent of people use Google to find information online every day. People *are* Googling your company. For example, I did a search for one of my industrial clients. As of this writing (a holiday week), their brand name appeared in 669 Google searches and their website received 337 total clicks from that over a seven-day period. That's almost 100 people each day making a Google search related to their brand name!

In addition, keep in mind that it's not just your own website or content that they will find. Word-of-mouth is not what it used to be. Just 10 years ago, upset customers or raving fans could spread their opinion about your business only to their family, friends, neighbors and work colleagues. Now, thanks to social networking and the infinite publishing power of the Web, customers can share their rants and raves instantly with a worldwide audience.

You have an online brand whether you like it or not. What customers find when they search for you can have serious consequences for your business.

In such a connected world, your online image is everything. If your online image is poor or tarnished, it can have a huge impact on your business in multiple areas – not just marketing:

- **Lead generation:** Lead generation is critical for a healthy sales pipeline that feeds business growth. If your Google results are soured with negativity when prospective customers search for your business, are they going to want to contact you? They may see it as a red flag and look elsewhere before your salespeople even talk to them. Your pipeline will dry up.

- **Selling:** A shrinking pipeline will affect sales, but there is more to the story. Do you have salespeople on the phones and pounding the pavement? The prospective customers they reach will use Google to research your company, as well. Imagine this: a salesperson gives a dynamite presentation at your prospect's office. After the meeting, they shake hands and promise to follow up. The prospect returns to his desk and Googles your company name for more background information. If what they see does not match what your salesperson promised (be it negative reviews or just a poor representation of your offerings on your website), faith and goodwill will be lost and the deal will be in jeopardy.

- **Customer retention:** Even loyal customers can get spooked by what they see about your company online. What if your biggest customer Googles your company name to quickly grab your phone number for an invoice question and sees a bunch of negative results right underneath the listing for your website? Will they be tempted to click and see what's there?

- **Recruiting:** You need a great team of employees for your company to be successful. What if a candidate goes to your website to research your company before an interview and finds nothing but outdated information? What if they go to one of your company's social media accounts and find no posts since 2012? Will they think your company is thriving or stalling?

- **Financing:** Let's say you need some cash to pay for upgraded equipment. Investors and creditors have integrated online research into their due diligence. A negative online image may make raising capital more difficult. If your search results look iffy, those much needed dollars will be harder to come by.

What makes an online brand?

An online brand is difficult to define because it's really based on the opinion someone forms of your company when they see the information available about it on the Web. You can't control that for two key reasons:

- Information about your company will make its way online from sources other than you.

- You can put your proverbial best foot forward, but ultimately, how people perceive the information will determine their emotional and logical response to it.

While you can't control everything that a prospective customer can find out about you online or how they feel about your brand, you can influence it. You just have to know where to start.

There are three main aspects of your online brand to consider:

1. What you proactively put online

In the discovery phase of new projects, I often hear several phrases like "Our website displays a tagline we stopped using in 2012" or "We started selling this product a year ago, but it isn't on our website yet" or "We haven't updated our social media profiles since we created them. I don't even have the passwords for them." When I hear statements like this, I wonder how many prospective customers companies have lost over years of online idleness.

The good news is that what you proactively put online (i.e., your website and social media profiles) is the easiest aspect of online branding to control. The bad news is that it takes a lot of work. The balance of this book covers proven strategies for proactively managing your online brand. While implementing these strategies and evaluating your online image, repeatedly ask yourself the following questions:

- Would I be proud or worried if my salespeople carried an iPad and used my website as a presentation tool?

- Would I be glad or worried if one of my top customers looked at my Facebook or LinkedIn page?

- Would I be glad or worried if I knew my customers looked at my website after a sales call?

If any of the situations above worry you, your online brand is in trouble.

2. How Google displays third-party information about you online
Google your company name. What do you see?

While online branding is not all about Google, it's important because the search engine gives you the quickest, most reliable snapshot of the information available online about your company. Whether you like it or not, that's what your customers see. And what your customers see has a lot to do with what they think about you. That, in a nutshell, is your online brand.

If you're not sure how to judge your online brand snapshot on Google, here are some exercises to guide you.

First, look at the first page of results for a search on your company name. You can see my company's on the next page.

Can you quickly and easily identify your own website in the top few natural results? Ignore the paid results, labeled Ads, for now. (We will discuss them later when we look at your PPC strategy.) If the answer to the question is yes, you've passed the first test. If you're in the top spot, you're in great shape. If your answer is no, you've got some issues to work through. Some are easier to fix than others.

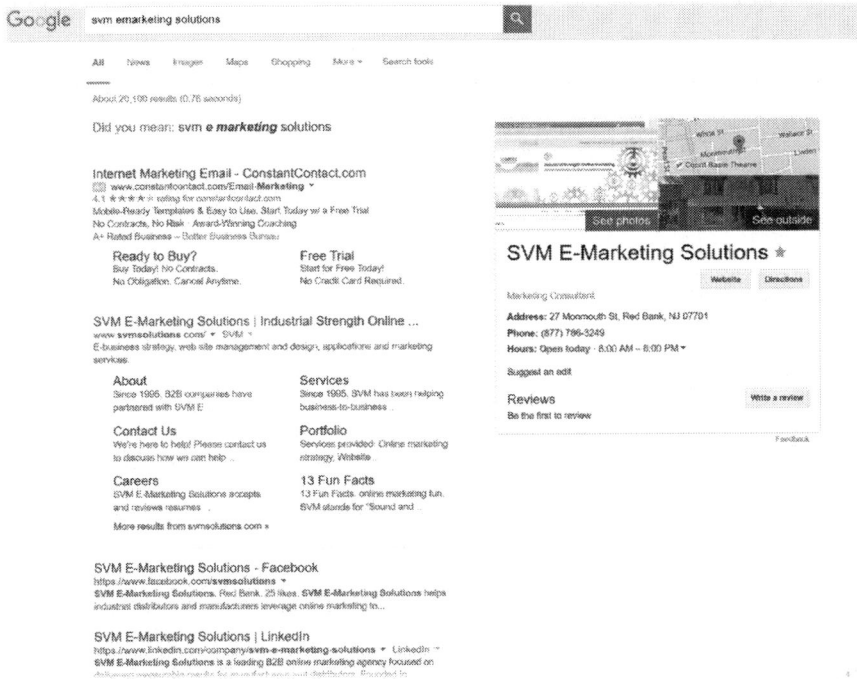

Assuming that you have a website (and if you don't, that should be the first challenge you tackle), is there some technical issue making it unreadable to search engines? Talk to your website provider or another professional and take care of it immediately.

Other issues may prove more difficult. Is your company name common or easily mistaken for another? Examples include acronyms or generic names, like Precision Tech. If other companies with similar names are well-known and/or optimized, you may have trouble getting that coveted first position.

What does the content in your website listing say about your company? Once you've found your listing, examine it closely. How does it portray your company? Are there links to internal pages?

While Google ultimately determines what it displays in your search listing, you can give your company its best possible chance of a good brand representation with good metadata, a well-defined SEO-friendly site structure and more. For help, see Chapter 7.

Do you see a Knowledge Graph near your listing? A Knowledge Graph is Google's way of displaying the information a searcher could want to know about a query, if the search engine is relatively certain of the searcher's intent. This includes branded searches for a specific company name.

The placement of a Knowledge Graph and how it looks depends on which device you used to Google search. On a desktop computer, you'll likely see it on the right (as pictured in the example for a search of "svm emarketing solutions.") On mobile devices, it's on top.

You cannot control whether or not Google displays a Knowledge Graph for a branded search of your company name. This is because they are formed from a multitude of sources, including Wikipedia, Google+ pages and more. There are also other mitigating factors, including the location of the searcher and the exact query used. Large companies (especially publicly traded ones) have a better chance of having a Wikipedia page – and therefore a Knowledge Graph – because they meet Wikipedia's notability requirements for a published article about them. But if your Google+ page is well optimized, this could help show valuable infor-mation like your phone number and operating hours within Google's search results. It will be harder to get a Knowledge Graph if you have a common company name because it makes searchers' intents for branded searches less clear to Google.

Do you "own" the first page for a search for your company name? How many listings other than the one for your own website are related to your company? While this is impossible to control because other third parties that mention your brand name are eligible to appear in Google results for the term, you can influence it.

Likely candidates to appear on a first search result page for your com-pany name include your social profiles (Facebook, LinkedIn, YouTube, Twitter, etc.), directory and review sites where your company is men-tioned (Yelp, Manta, etc.), partner sites (manufacturers, distributors or vendors) and places where you've published or have had content published about you (job sites, news outlets, industry publications, etc.).

By creating something relevant that you know will rank well in Google's algorithm (a LinkedIn company page, if you don't already have one), you've got a good chance of having it pop up on the first page.

Has anything negative been written about you? This area has the most potential to be damaging to your online brand. Google seeks information from review sites to include in the search results and often includes visual representations of numerical ratings in the form of stars.

While ratings and reviews are more common in the B2C arena, they are present in the B2B arena, as well. For example, if customers have written reviews and given you a numerical rating on your Facebook page, that is eligible to show up in your search results with your Facebook page listing.

3. How you respond and relate to what other say about you online

While you can't control exactly what third-party reviews, ratings and information Google shows, you can influence your customers' perception of them by how you respond.

At the beginning of this chapter, I referenced a quote from Jeff Bezos, founder of Amazon: "Your brand is what people say about you when you're not in the room." When people search for your company online, you are most definitely not in the room, which means you can't explain anything.

But many third-party sites (like review sites and social media outlets) give business owners a chance to respond when someone writes something about their company, positive or negative. Even though the original review, comment or mention won't be erased, other people who see it will also be able to see the resulting interaction that occurred. That could make all the difference in how your company is perceived.

The first step is making sure that you know what is said about you online in a timely manner. To do so, create a brand-monitoring strategy.

Identify key phrases that represent your company so you can track when they pop up online. Consider:

- Company name
- Brand names
- Product names
- Key executive and employee names
- Taglines and mottos

If you want to find out what people are saying about your competitors and your industry at the same time, consider including:

- All of the above for your competitors
- Important industry keywords

Once you've identified the phrases to track, put a process in place to monitor them on a regular basis. You can do this manually by performing Google searches or you can use tools to automate it, including Google Alerts, Social Mention, Hootsuite, Klout, Twitter Search, Viralheat and Sprout Social. Also, make sure you create a culture where your employees can speak up if they see or hear something about your company's brand.

Once you have a process in place and you're monitoring your image at regular intervals, put a plan of action in place to respond consistently when someone says something about your company (positive or negative).

If the mention is positive: Perhaps one of your customers is talking about a good experience they had with one of your employees, products or services; find a way to acknowledge it. This can signal to prospective customers and other parties that you care about your reputation, your people and your business. Whether it's a simple thank you, a "like" or a reply, acknowledgment of positive mentions will enhance your online brand.

If the mention is negative: Maybe it's a customer sounding off about a recent interaction with your company or a disgruntled employee complaining that he was let go. First of all, don't panic. You may be tempted to respond immediately to defend your company and your position, but don't act in haste. While quick response is necessary, make sure that your anger and emotions are in check before you do anything. Consult trustworthy colleagues or partners, and run your response plan by them. Also, consider where you will respond. If you get a negative review on a third-party or social media site, think about contacting the customer directly to work out the specifics of an issue. Provide a short response on the site itself to say that you've contacted them to make things right. This will prevent you from "airing dirty laundry" in a public forum while still letting you acknowledge to future viewers of the review that you've done your best to resolve an issue.

If the mention is neutral: Is a customer requesting a product or service enhancement? Are they asking a question about a resource you posted online (like a whitepaper or blog post)? This type of response can be an opportunity. Use it to converse with your customers openly, and you may be surprised at what comes out of the interaction.

No matter what, listen. Be sure to consider each mention carefully and keep track of feedback trends. If people are continually saying some specific thing, take it seriously and do what you need to do to fix it.

Remember: Having an online brand is not optional

You have an online brand, whether you like it or not. It's not optional! And you can't afford to ignore it. With proactive, strategic effort leveraging many of the tactics detailed in this book, you can influence and shape how your customers see your company. If you build a solid online brand, more people will want to do business with you. And that will give you good return on your online marketing and branding investment.

Chapter 5
Become a Content Marketer

To effectively market your products and services today, do not rely exclusively on marketing your products and services. There are a number of reasons people choose to do business with you besides having the right product at the right price. They might appreciate the way your company stands behind its products or they might enjoy the relationship you've created with them. Establishing your company or individuals and teams within your company as experts or specialists adds great value to customer perception and your relationship. They'll choose to do business with you because of your specialized knowledge about the applications and best practices for the product.

So market your specialized knowledge to demonstrate to prospects and customers that you are the expert in your field. Leading with your specialized knowledge – or keeping free, useful content in front of customers – is key to successful marketing in the 21st century.

In other words, you need to become a content marketer.

Content marketing is the creation and distribution of relevant and valuable content to attract, acquire and engage clearly defined target audiences with the goal of driving action. Content marketing needs to serve as the cornerstone of your online marketing strategy. Create educational items that are interesting and useful to your target audience and turn your website into a resource center. While this is a time-intensive endeavor, the benefits will far outweigh the cost. The following are proven content marketing vehicles that should form the backbone of your content marketing efforts.

Blog posts: Blog posts are insightful and timely Web content that highlight important news, observations, tips and other useful content. Readers of your posts are encouraged to share their comments, allowing for a two-way dialogue. Blog posts offer a great opportunity to keep your website current and relevant through short 250- to 500-word posts. Blogs themselves are essentially one-page websites that are simple and inexpensive to set up.

Articles: By creating 500- to 1,000-word educational articles that demonstrate a best practice or little-known insight, you can showcase your expertise and demonstrate to your customers that you understand their needs.

Whitepapers: Whitepapers are topical, educational reports or guides oriented toward a particular industry challenge, opportunity or best practice. Generally, whitepapers are five to 15 pages in length and help you demonstrate thought leadership on issues that are important to your customers.

E-books: E-books are lengthier than whitepapers, generally ranging from 55 to 100 pages in length, and present complex information in a compelling and entertaining way.

Videos: If a picture is worth a thousand words, a video is worth a million. Use online video to demonstrate a product, illustrate a best practice, allow customers to see your company behind the scenes, etc. Online videos do not have to be professionally produced – an inexpensive digital camera will work well. The key is to film content your customers will find useful and actionable or that will bolster their sense of who you are to help build a relationship with them.

Presentations: PowerPoint or similar software can be used to create educational presentations oriented toward a particular challenge, opportunity or best practice. Presentations can be five to 50 pages in length – whatever it takes to make your point.

Webinars: A webinar is a seminar that is conducted over the Web that participants can easily view from their office or home – either live or on-demand. Most webinars include a visual slide presentation, as well as an audio broadcast that is accessed either over the computer or phone. Webinars should range from 30 to 90 minutes with some time allocated to questions and answers.

I know what you're thinking: "Bob, you're out of your mind! There is no possible way for me to create this much content. I'm too busy running my business." I hear this all the time when I present this concept. The good news is that it's not that difficult. First, you don't need to create the content yourself. You can find many talented and reasonably priced writers on Upwork (upwork.com) or Guru (guru.com) to help you. Second, you can produce many content items easily by embracing the concept of repurposing. If you can come up with one good idea that your customers will find valuable, you can create multiple content types based on that idea and/or content and reuse it across several marketing vehicles.

Here's an example of repurposing content from my business. A number of years ago, search engine marketing became a hot topic that business leaders wanted to embrace, but it was overly confusing. I knew there was a proven, seven-step process for search engine marketing success, so I wrote a 750-word article, "Seven Steps to Search Engine Marketing Success," which I published on my website, as well as in association newsletters and industry publications. It was very successful, so I wrote a whitepaper with the same title. The content is the same, only presented in a more detailed, 18-page format. I use the whitepaper on my website as a lead generator. Interested people can download the whitepaper for free in exchange for their basic contact information. I also created how-to videos, webinars and live presentations based on the same idea.

All you need to do is come up with one good idea per month and you can create five content items based on that idea. At the end of a year, you will have 60 valuable content items in your content marketing arsenal.

Brainstorm great content ideas

The first, if not the most difficult, step in content marketing is figuring out what you're going to write about. If you've ever tried to write anything, I'm sure you've had episodes of writer's block – staring at the blank page for what seems like an eternity hoping for creative inspiration. Successful content marketers don't have this problem because they are always on the lookout for new and innovative content ideas. Put these tips into action and you won't have this problem either.

Follow industry news. The key to creating timely, relevant content is to be plugged into the latest news and trends in your industry. Get in the habit of reading online publications and blogs in your industry. Google Alerts (google.com/alerts) can help automate this process by emailing you whenever industry news is published.

Monitor social conversations. What are people tweeting about on Twitter, posting on Facebook or discussing on LinkedIn? These social conversations can be a great source for content ideas. Follow LinkedIn groups, Twitter feeds and Facebook pages related to your industry. You can automate this process using services like Hootsuite (hootsuite.com) to monitor social conversations.

Ask your sales and service people. Your salespeople and customer service people are interacting with your customers on a daily basis and know their needs, challenges and opportunities. I bet there's a treasure trove of content ideas there. These people do not need to be great writers; ask them for the raw meat of each content idea. A talented copywriter can turn their raw meat into a brilliantly written piece.

Ask your customers. To be effective, your content needs to be customer-focused. When brainstorming content ideas, why not ask your best customers for input? Conduct an online survey asking your customers to let you know their top challenges and questions. You are sure to get some great content ideas.

Conduct original research. By conducting original research, you'll have content that is uniquely yours. Create a brief, focused survey on a topic your customers find important. Once you compile your results, analyze them and look for trends and insights. This valuable data can be used for many blog posts and articles. You can also publish a study of all the results as a whitepaper.

Eavesdrop on email conversations with customers. Now this may seem too Big Brother for some, but it is an effective way to understand the questions your customers have about your products, services and solutions. By setting up your email system to automatically BCC (blind carbon copy – yes, an old-fashioned term that's been repurposed on the Internet) your salespeople's messages, you will be able to see the questions that your customers are asking, as well as the valuable answers your salespeople provide. By mining the information in these conversations, you will come up with countless content ideas.

Repurpose great content. As mentioned earlier, this is one of my favorite ways of coming up with content ideas. Did you write an article that got great feedback? Write a 10-page whitepaper on the same subject. Film a short video blog. Create a webinar. Each good idea you come up with can be leveraged to create multiple content types.

Consider evergreen content. Evergreen content is content that stays useful for years with little or no need for upkeep. It can be referenced long after it was first created and still provides great value to the reader. What information or topics could you write about that will always be in season?

Map content to the buying process

Now that you have all of this great content in a variety of different formats, it's time to put everything to work in your marketing and sales processes. Not only can this content be a great resource to help generate leads on your website, but your salespeople can leverage this content to nurture relationships with prospects and convert leads into sales.

There are three primary steps in the buying process, and your marketing and sales teams can strategically lead prospects through the process by sharing appropriate content at each step.

- **Stage 1 – Awareness:** At this stage, the prospect identifies a problem or an opportunity. Content that will help your prospects increase the awareness of their need includes: blog posts, articles, email newsletters and social media updates.

- **Stage 2 – Research:** After the prospect realizes they have the need, they begin to research possible solutions. They commit to change and begin looking for possible providers. Content that will help your prospects increase the awareness of their need includes: how-to guides, webinars, whitepapers and how-to/demonstration videos.

- **Stage 3 – Decision:** The content used to nurture prospects through the first two stages should have landed your business on the short list. Now it's time to use your content to demonstrate to prospects that you are the best choice to fill their need. Content that will help your prospects increase the awareness of their need includes: case studies, written and video testimonials, ROI articles and calculators, and animated or video demonstrations.

Think like a publisher: Create an editorial calendar

Content marketing may seem like a daunting task, especially since you need to run many other aspects of your business. The good news is that you can make this process manageable by thinking like a publisher and establishing an editorial calendar.

Publishers of magazines don't sit down each month and say: "Hmmm, what should we write about this month?" They plan 12 to 24 months in advance. This allows them to efficiently manage the content creation process and provides plenty of lead time. I recommend you leverage this same proven process.

Brainstorm content ideas with your team and map them out on a calendar, taking into account seasonal aspects of your business, holidays or major events. Then, delegate content creation responsibilities well in advance so there is plenty of time to create great content your customers will love.

As you get more sophisticated with your content marketing, you can make your editorial calendar more targeted, focusing on content marketing tactics that should be performed daily, weekly, monthly and quarterly.

Remember, you have specialized and valuable knowledge and insights about your products, services, industry and more. Creating content to engage, inform and build relationships with your customers in places and ways that are meaningful to them isn't rocket science. The less tech-savvy you are, the more you might rely on the skills of those in your company who can do this stuff in their sleep. If your customers are getting younger, chances are your employees are too. Tap their built-in knowledge and experience for both creating and disseminating content.

Daily content marketing tactics:	Weekly content marketing tactics:
• Respond to comments on your blog • Post LinkedIn status updates featuring a previous article • Tweet a link to a previous whitepaper on your Twitter feed • Post a Facebook page update featuring a previous video	• Create a new blog post • Write a new how-to article • Post an update in LinkedIn Groups featuring a previous article • Respond to a LinkedIn status update
Monthly content marketing tactics:	**Quarterly content marketing tactics:**
• Record a new how-to video • Send an email newsletter featuring your newest content this month • Write a new case study • Write a new how-to guide	• Publish a new whitepaper • Record customer testimonial videos • Produce a webinar • Create an e-book

Chapter 6

Make Your Website the Hub of Your Marketing

To be a successful 21st century marketer, you must understand that your website is not a separate marketing channel. Your website should serve as the hub of your marketing efforts, where traffic from search engines, direct mail, print ads, email, online directories, social media and public relations eventually arrive or pass through. By approaching your website this way, you gain the following advantages:

- **You can communicate an unlimited marketing message.** There is only so much information that you can communicate in a print ad or postcard. By directing viewers to your website, you can extend that marketing message in an engaging way.

- **Your website allows for two-way communication.** Unlike offline marketing tools that are static, one-way communication tools, your website can provide opportunities for customers or prospects to interact and engage with you in real time.

- **Your marketing becomes measurable.** By making your website the hub of all marketing, you can easily measure the results and return on investment for all of your marketing activities, including your offline efforts.

Unfortunately, most manufacturers and distributors do not approach their websites this way, with many offering little more than a glorified brochure. This chapter will show you how to transform your website into a powerful marketing tool that your customers (and salespeople) will love.

Be customer-focused, not egocentric

This may sound like a ridiculous statement, but all too often companies do not design their websites for their customers. Rather, they take an egocentric approach to Web design, more interested in talking about their own products, history, news or events than their customers' needs and wants. While that information may be important to you, it's not necessarily what your customers are interested in.

People are not visiting your website to kill time. They are visiting to find a solution, answer a question or take the next step to do business with you. To be successful, create a website for your customers, not you. If your website does not serve your prospects and customers, it will not serve you either.

A customer-focused website puts your customers at the center of your online offering, making it easy for them to do business with you. At the same time, a customer-focused website is aligned with your company's overall business strategy and marketing objectives. Most importantly, a customer-focused website produces results: leads, sales and profitable long-term customers. How can you make your website customer-focused?

- **Speak directly to each member of your target audience.** To create a customer-focused website, you need to know who your most profitable customers are. By clearly identifying your niche target audiences, you can speak directly to their unique needs and motivations.

- **Provide content and features that address your customers' needs.** A customer-focused website anticipates your customers' needs and provides the solutions they seek.

- **Educate and build trust.** Your website cannot just sell; it must also educate. A customer-focused website serves as a vital resource your customers cannot live without by offering educational articles, guides, videos and other content that helps your customers become more informed.

- **Persuade visitors to take action.** A customer-focused website does not take a passive approach toward generating leads and sales. It offers a variety of calls to action throughout the website to convert anonymous visitors into named leads for your sales process.

- **Makes it easy for customers to do business with you.** A customer-focused website serves as the hub of all your marketing activities and provides customers and prospects with an interactive and dynamic way to conduct business with you.

Create a customer-focused website strategy

Have you seriously considered the strategic role of your website? Once you do, you will be on the path toward creating your most powerful marketing tool. An effective website can help you achieve a number of business goals, such as generating leads, building a marketing database, enhancing customer service and selling online. However, to produce results online, you must align your website objectives with your overall marketing and business objectives.

The creation of an effective website involves careful consideration of a wide range of strategic, creative and technical issues including:

- **Your website's goals and objectives.** Before creating a new website or enhancing an existing one, it is important to step back and take a broad view of your company's goals and objectives. An effective website can help you achieve a number of business goals. Some examples include: attracting new customers, selling online, enhancing customer service, improving sales force productivity and educating audiences.

- **Your most profitable customers.** It shouldn't be a surprise that to create a customer-focused website you need to carefully consider your customers. Consider your niche markets discussed in Chapter 3. Analyze these markets to identify your most profitable customer segments. Carefully consider their needs, motivations and why they do business with you. Each of these areas will help identify their motive for visiting your website.

- **Your competition.** I consider the Web to be the great equalizer because it levels the playing field by providing companies – even small companies – with the opportunity to compete against their largest competitor. An effectively designed website can make a small company look large and dominant; a poorly designed website can make even a large, successful company look small and insignificant. It is important that your website stand out among your competitors. Spend some time reviewing your competitors' websites to identify opportunities to shine – you can learn a lot from their online successes and failures.

- **Your success measures.** To be successful with online marketing, you need to be able to accurately measure the bottom-line impact your website is having on your business. Examples of quantifiable success measures include:

  - **Web traffic:** How many new and returning visitors came to our website?

  - **Traffic sources:** What are the best sources of profitable traffic to my website?

  - **Conversions:** Is my website converting anonymous visitors into leads and sales?

  - **Customer acquisition cost:** What am I paying per conversion and is it reasonable based on my product/service gross margins?

Create customer-focused content and features

With your customer-focused website strategy now in place, it is time to create compelling content and features that will make your company stand out as the obvious choice. It is important for you to leverage the latest online marketing best practices when identifying customer-focused content and crafting copy your customers will love.

Don't just grab your latest brochures and slap this content on your website. Too many companies cop out by taking this approach, and they end up with a lackluster website.

Instead, make your website appeal to your customers' needs and motivations. As stated earlier, your customers are not visiting your website to kill time. They are visiting to serve a need or find a solution. Think carefully about your customers' motivation for visiting your website. What are they looking for? What do they hope to accomplish?

Based on your customers' unique needs and motivations, identify content and features that speak to the needs of your customers and provide the solution they are seeking. When a prospect is considering a product or service for their needs, they have a number of key questions in their minds. Demonstrate that you understand the challenges they face and offer a solution. When creating your customer-focused content, answer the following questions:

- Why would a customer choose your business over a competitor?

- What differentiates your product or service offering from the competition, and what benefit is served by a customer choosing you? As a marketing friend of mine says, "It's USP meets WIIFM."[1]

- What visual examples will help convey the quality and value of your products or services (e.g., photos, videos, testimonials, etc.)?

- What informational resources do you have that answer questions about your products or services (e.g., whitepapers, videos, FAQs, etc.)?

- What information will help customers feel confident about your skills and experience (e.g., certifications, testimonials, customer ratings, licenses, years of experience, etc.)?

- What can you offer to eliminate risk and shorten the sales cycle (e.g., guarantees, free trials, free consultations, etc.)?

Create customer-focused copy

Companies often think their website is designed to serve the thousands of people who will visit it, when the reality is you should strive to connect with each visitor by using a friendly, conversational tone in your copy.

---

1   Unique selling position meets "What's in it for me?"

Keep your sentences short and to the point. Conversational sentences should be no more than 10 to 15 words. A shorter sentence structure makes for an easier read and sounds more inviting and relaxed. In addition, make sure your thoughts flow together.

Speak to the reader. Write as though you're sitting with them over coffee. Use a conversational tone. Words like "you," "your" and "we" give it a personal feel.

Avoid jargon, buzzwords and internal company-speak. Don't assume that your reader has an understanding of jargon or industry terminology. Use simple terms, assuming your readers know nothing about the subject, without being condescending.

Write content that is easy to scan. People scan Web pages before they read them in detail, so make your Web content short and easy to scan by using bullet points and bold text for headings and by breaking your content into logical chunks.

Read your copy out loud. While you're writing your website copy, read it out loud. Make sure it sounds natural, as if you are speaking personally with your readers. If it doesn't, go back and polish the rough edges.

Package your Web content for success

Great Web content alone is not enough to engage your customers. Your content must be packaged in an appealing and accessible way to encourage visitors to read on and dig deeper. Leverage contemporary Web packaging techniques to ensure your content does its job.

Make strategic use of your home page. First impressions count and more people will see your home page than any other page on your website, make it as welcoming and useful as possible. You have less than five seconds to make a positive impression. Make sure you appeal to prospects and draw them in.

Clearly communicate who you are and the audiences you serve. Clearly present your capabilities on your home page, including:

- The products and services you sell

- The most common applications for your products or services

- The industries or businesses you serve

- The geographical areas you serve

But don't get bogged down in detail. This information can be conveyed through headers, links and images. For example, you don't want to list all of your locations on the home page, but you may consider a map that highlights the area you serve.

Design paths through your website. Focus on your customers' needs and offer paths that guide visitors through your website to find the information that will best help them.

Feature information that can be found deeper in the site. Your home page should provide a timely digest of the latest and greatest information you have to offer. Use it to feature products, services, news, educational resources, blog posts, etc.

Update your home page often. People want to do business with dynamic and active companies. The best way to demonstrate this is by having a dynamic and active home page.

Make your website easy to navigate. When creating your website, make sure customers can find their way around your site. Intuitive navigation is essential so that people can find what they want quickly and easily. If they can't, they may get frustrated and leave for your competitor's site. The following best practices will help ensure your customers can easily find their way around your website.

Organize information into logical buckets. To make information easy to find, begin by organizing your content into logical buckets. Most B2B websites will have the following primary buckets of content:

- Products and/or services
- Customers served
- Applications/industries
- Educational resources
- Customer service/support
- News and events
- About the company
- Contact

Offer a consistent primary and subnavigation on every page. Navigation should be presented consistently on every page of your website, including the home page. Present primary navigation horizontally at the top of every page of your site and subnavigation vertically on the left-hand side of every page.

Provide "breadcrumb trail" navigation to show the visitor's path. A "breadcrumb trail" is an alternative text-based navigation tool that reveals the visitor's location in your website. The term comes from the fairy tale *Hansel and Gretel* in which the children drop breadcrumbs to mark a trail back to their home. Just like in the story, a breadcrumb trail below the primary navigation in your website offers visitors a way to trace the path back to their original point of entry.

Offer a sitewide search engine. A search engine is often the navigation item of last resort. If people cannot find what they are looking for by browsing, they will turn to search. Integrate a capable search engine into the top right of every page on your website. Also, use a search engine that can log website searches. By keeping track of site search behavior, you will uncover content that is either difficult for customers to find or missing from your site entirely.

Provide text links to related sections. Don't organize your content into navigation silos. In addition to the navigation methods described above, provide appropriate text-based navigation aids in logical spots in your website's copy. You want to provide customers with a variety of ways to find the content they are interested in.

Merchandise your products and services. Online merchandising is all about presenting your products and services in a customer-focused manner to encourage engagement and conversions. The key to effective merchandising is to align your products and services content as closely as possible with the customer's needs.

Remember the 80-20 rule. For many companies, 80 percent of their sales come from 20 percent of their product or service offering. Lead with your top 20 percent when featuring products on your website and you'll serve the widest audience.

Logically organize your products. Group your products and services into categories based on how they are used and what other products are most often used with them.

Present detailed product and service pages. On your product pages, offer everything a customer would need to make an informed decision. Give detailed, customer-focused product descriptions.

Use compelling product images. Images provide the first impression of your product. They should be of extremely high quality and placed above the scroll so customers can see them without scrolling.

Complement images with video. Since customers can't touch or test a product on your website, a video is the best way to present its value. Film product demonstration videos and video blogs where you describe the value of your product or service. Zappos, the massive online clothing retailer, found that sales increased up to 30 percent for items that included video product demonstrations.

Allow customers to rate and review products. Customer reviews are a proven driver of sales. The majority of customers will want to see what their peers think about a product before deciding to make a purchase.

Showcase your knowledge in an educational resource center. Your website should not just sell, it should also educate. Put your content marketing arsenal to work and complement your product and service information with valuable educational content that helps your customers do their jobs better.

Create a "Resource Center" on your website. Offer your educational content in a resource or learning center. Pack it with your how-to articles, best practice guides, videos and other educational content. This will turn your website into a resource that customers will visit regularly because it is so helpful.

Link to related educational content from product and service pages. Don't create content silos, presenting educational content and product information exclusively in their own sections. Create links from product and service pages to related educational content and vice versa.

Update your educational content on a regular basis. Improve the value of your resource center by creating and publishing new educational content frequently. Remember, you're a content marketer.

Turn your website into a lead-generation and sales machine. Lead generation consistently ranks as a top priority for B2B companies. However, most companies handicap themselves by relying on their website's Contact Us page as the sole method for prospects to take action. Don't make this mistake. Proactively turn your website into a lead generation and sales machine.

Make an offer they can't refuse. Only 10 percent of your website visitors are ready to buy; the other 90 percent are kicking tires, performing research or nursing a presales question. To turn your website into a lead generation machine, present a variety of offers that appeal to prospects at different stages of the purchasing cycle. This will help you generate leads for near-term business, as well as build a marketing database to nurture future opportunities.

Successful B2B offers have these characteristics:

- **High perceived value** – Your customers and prospects place a significant monetary or emotional value on your offer and want to take advantage of it.

- **Highly desirable** – The offer is so valuable, your customers and prospects want to take advantage of it right now.

- **Uniquely yours** – Your offer is unique to your company and cannot be found anywhere else.

- **Related to the value of your offering** – Your offer is a first step that leads your customers and prospects toward the ultimate sale.

- **Easy to respond to** – People do not have to jump through hoops to respond to your offer. Provide a simple process for them to take the next step.

- **Minimizes risk or obligation** – By taking advantage of your offer, you make customers and prospects more comfortable doing business with you.

Examples of successful B2B offers include:

- **Request More Info** – A basic offer for people who want more information about your product, service or company.

- **Request a Quote** or **Add to Cart** – These offers are tailored for the 10 percent of people who are ready to buy from you.

- **Download Whitepaper** – People will give up basic contact information to download your whitepapers and guides.

- **Watch Webinar** – As with whitepapers and guides, people will give up basic contact information in exchange for information.

- **Subscribe to Newsletter** – An email newsletter sign-up is a nice, low-threat offer that will appeal to early-stage prospects.

- **Free Trial** – If you can offer a free trial of your product or service, you can minimize risk by making it easier for prospects to want to buy.

- **Free Samples** – As with free trials, free samples minimize risk by letting prospects sample the goods.

- **Free Consultation** – This works well if you offer professional services.

- **Enter Contest** – People love to win things, but just because they entered your contest doesn't mean they want to do business with you. While this offer works, it does not deliver the most targeted leads.

- **Ask a Question** – This offer delivers targeted prospects. It's a nice low-threat call to action that early-stage prospects will take advantage of because they don't assume they are starting a sales conversation.

Just like in real estate, location matters for your call to action. There is a reason Amazon places the Add to Cart box in the upper right-hand section of every page: *It works!* Do the same thing and you will be amazed by how many more prospects reach out to you because you make it easy for them.

Design your forms to generate leads and sales. Most of your calls to action will send people to complete an online form. You may not realize it, but your Web forms may be hurting your lead generation efforts. Most online forms are too long, too hidden or too unpersuasive to generate leads – but you need them to fill your sales pipeline.

- **Use a simple and clean design.** Make your forms appear easy to complete by leveraging white space to improve legibility, removing all unnecessary elements and ensuring that your field labels are understandable.

- **Remove unnecessary fields.** The more fields your forms include, the less likely prospects will be to fill them out. Ask only for basic contact information and product interests that your salespeople will need to make an intelligent follow-up (e.g., name, company, phone, email and product interest).

- **Fix your buttons.** Label your buttons so they represent the action the prospect wants to take; no one wants to "submit." Use phrases like Order Now, Sign Up, Begin Free Trial, Request a Quote, Please Contact Me, etc. Also, use large buttons with contrasting colors so the button pops off the page.

- **Get creative – use the Mad Libs approach.** Try offering your lead generation form in a narrative format, presenting input fields to people as blanks within sentences. It is a fun and interesting way for prospects to take the next step.

- **Get creative – ask a question.** Replace your field labels with complete questions, such as "How many do you want to buy?" instead of "Quantity." It makes your form friendlier and easier to understand.

- **Simplify your checkout process.** Cut the number of clicks required to complete the sale. Communicate shipping costs early. Offer a progress meter to let people know where they are in the process. In addition, offer alternative (offline) ways to order.

- **Provide a nurturing offer on your Thank You pages.** After someone completes an online form, they should be presented with a confirmation page that thanks them for their efforts. These pages offer a great opportunity to nurture prospects further through the pipeline. According to MarketingSherpa,[2] 39 percent of prospects accept offers on thank you pages, so this is a great time to offer your e-newsletter, social media follows or discount on a future purchase.

---

2   Holland, Anne, "39% of Viewers Accept Offers on 'Thank You' Pages," MarketingSherpa LLC, Jan. 29. 2007, https://www.marketingsherpa.com/article/blog/39-viewers-accept-offers-on

Prominently display your phone number. Even with the growth of Generation Net, many people still prefer to pick up the phone and call while they are on a website. To boost the number of inquiries you receive, don't make your visitors hunt for your phone number. Make your phone number one of the prominent calls to action on every page of your website and encourage prospects to call you. Since they can use the website as a presentation tool, there is no better time for your salespeople to be speaking with prospects.

I recommend using a unique toll-free number on your website so you can accurately track the number of calls you receive from website visitors. This will help you close the loop in terms of tracking inbound leads from your website.

Offer online chat as an alternative to phone and forms. My clients are having great success offering online chat as an alternative to a phone number and online forms. Many are receiving 10 times more chats than online form completions. By calling you, a prospect will get an immediate response, but not everyone is ready to engage in a sales conversation. By using an online form, prospects can remain somewhat anonymous, but they assume it will take hours or days before they get a response. Online chat offers the best of both worlds. Prospects can get an immediate response while retaining a measure of anonymity.

It's very easy to integrate online chat into your website. Hosted chat services like LivePerson (liveperson.com) offer an intuitive tool set for integrating chat buttons onto your site, as well as a Web-based interface for managing chat conversations. You can populate the system with answers to frequently asked questions and have multiple chatters involved in the process. For example, a receptionist could serve the front-line triage role managing all incoming chats. As hot leads come in, the chat can be transferred to a knowledgeable salesperson to continue the discussion.

Most business leaders mistakenly assume online chat must be available 24 hours a day, 365 days a year. You can offer online chat only during your normal business hours and still be effective. When you start the day, open the chat program and the chat option will become available on your site. At the end of the day, close the program and chat will no longer be available.

Shorten the follow-up time. Whatever method you use to generate leads, make sure you have a process in place to shorten the follow-up time. How long does it currently take for your salespeople to follow up on online lead inquiries? If the follow-up is not immediate, you are leaving money on the table.

It is absolutely shocking how many companies hurt their online lead generation efforts because they have a poor follow-up process. According to a study performed by *Harvard Business Review*[3]:

- 37 percent of companies respond to their leads within an hour.

- 16 percent respond within one to 24 hours.

- 24 percent of companies take more than 24 hours.

- 23 percent of companies never respond at all to their online leads.

Almost one-quarter of companies **never** respond to online leads. Another quarter is taking more than a day to respond to an interested prospect. All of the money and time invested in generating the lead is completely lost due to poor or missing follow-up. What a waste!

Don't make this vital mistake. Assign salespeople to follow up on online leads and make sure the inquiries get to them as soon as possible. Also, don't let leads languish in someone's inbox. Look for technology solutions to shorten the follow-up time. Tie your website forms into a customer relationship management system like Salesforce.com (salesforce.com), SugarCRM (sugarcrm.com) or Infusionsoft (infusionsoft.com) to streamline your lead management and follow-up process. You can also take a low-tech route and direct online and phone-in leads to a salesperson's smartphone. The goal is to make sure your salespeople talk to the prospect when they are still on your website, so they can use your website as a presentation tool.

---

3   Oldroyd, James B., Kristina McElheran and David Elkington, "The Short Life of Online Sales Leads," Harvard Business Review, March 2011, https://hbr.org/2011/03/the-short-life-of-online-sales-leads

Effective websites are no longer the massive, stand alone brochures they once were. Done correctly and integrated with your other marketing vehicles, your website can and will generate new business, support sustainable relationships with existing customers, measure the success of your efforts, engage and inform customers and prospects, and help your salespeople be more effective.

What's more, the cost of creating a great website, and of making updates and changes to your site, is going down. Please don't overlook this critical tool to marketing success in the 21st century.

Chapter 7
Help Customers Find You

You're sitting at your desk staring at a sheet of paper with names and numbers on it. Several have been crossed out, a couple have been circled, and there are notes jotted in the margins that say things like "WCB," "on vacation" or "doesn't work there anymore." You've been faithfully making calls for several hours with little or nothing to show for it except a slight headache and a kink in your shoulder from holding the phone (on a cord) against your ear. Just another day of trying to prevent prospects from running for the hills when they hear the phone ring. The good ol' days, right?

The days of the cold call may be coming to an end. For one thing, techniques for qualifying leads have improved enormously. Just Google "how to qualify a lead." My recent search yielded more than 51 million results! For another, caller ID and the well-honed skills of front office staff mean that your call may be ignored or tagged as a sales call before you ever talk to anyone. But more importantly, these days it's not about tracking down people and hounding them with phone calls; it's about creating ways for them to find you and connect on their terms.

In some ways, sales and marketing are more interconnected than ever before. One of the key differences between the way things are and the way they were has to do with how relationships are formed with prospects. Today, it's marketing that creates a relationship with a prospect, often before the sales team ever even hears about the prospect. The role of the sales closer is still relevant, but how you get to that point is what has changed.

Generation Net doesn't want to talk to you until they have a need for your products or services. In 80 percent of B2B transactions today the customer finds the supplier, not the other way around, according to research from MarketingSherpa[1]. And the vast majority of people are turning to search engines like Google or Bing to find the best supplier. These search engines use complicated algorithms and other formulas for ranking websites and content that people are searching for. The higher you rank (the closer you are to the top of the first page of results), the more likely people are to find you and click on your link. So it is critical for you to add search engine marketing to your marketing mix.

Unfortunately, many people don't engage in search engine marketing because they find it to be overly confusing. This chapter is designed to clear up that confusion and put you on the path to search engine marketing success.

What is search engine marketing?

Search engine marketing is the art and science of attracting motivated customers to your website by increasing your website's presence within the search results of the major search engines (i.e., Google, Bing and Yahoo). Search engine marketing is important because 72 percent of B2B customers begin at a search engine when researching products and services online, according to research from Pardot.

Effective search engine marketing begins with a thorough understanding of the keyword phrases your customers search for most often, followed by leveraging a combination of search engine optimization and pay-per-click advertising to be found during those searches.

Search engine optimization

Organic search engine optimization, also known as SEO, is the ongoing process of improving and promoting a website to increase the number of targeted visitors the site receives from search engines. The better optimized your website is, the higher the ranking it will achieve in the "organic" or "natural" search engine results. About 75 percent of searchers prefer to click on the organic results because they consider them

---

1   Adams, Dan, "Three Ways to Put Potential Customers to Work Pushing Your New B2B Product," American Management Association, Nov. 1, 2012, http://www.amanet.org/training/articles/Powered-by-Prospects.aspx

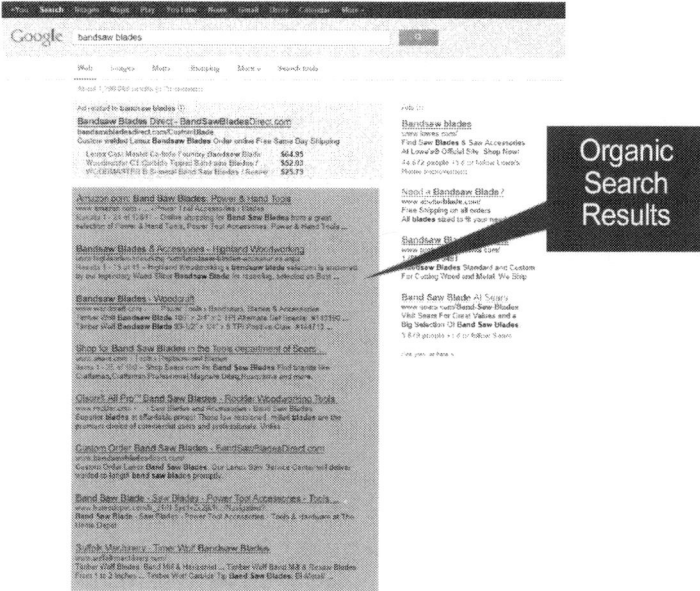

more genuine. Google dominates B2B searches with a 90 percent market share, according to research by Optify,[2] so most SEO campaigns focus on improving a site's ranking in Google.

Your SEO campaign should focus on getting your website on the first page of the search results. The higher you are listed on the page the better, since most searchers prefer to click on the first few links. You can accomplish this by focusing on the following two tactics:

- **Improve your website's relevance.** Your website needs to leverage your most important keyword phrases in a way that is relevant to your website's copy and coding. The more relevant your website is to what a person is searching, the higher your ranking will be in the organic search results. Note: The words or phrases you think might be the most relevant to prospects' searches may or may not be what they're using to find what you offer, something I'll explore later in this chapter.

---

2   "2012 B2B Marketing Benchmark Report," Optify, Jan. 23, 2013, http://www.slideshare.net/ScottValentine1/2012-b2b-markeng-benchmark-report

- **Improve your website's link popularity.** You need to attract quality inbound links to your website on an ongoing basis. An inbound link is a link into your website from a third-party website. The more quality links coming into your website, the higher your ranking will be in the search results. These days Google is placing a greater emphasis on link popularity over site relevancy when determining a site's ranking in the search results.

SEO is very similar to public relations: It requires an ongoing, consistent effort to achieve results. Significant results can be achieved within a three- to six-month time frame and will continue to build from there.

Pay-per-click advertising

With pay-per-click advertising, or PPC, your company pays a predetermined amount to have a text-based advertisement listed in the paid search results. However, you will only be charged when a searcher actually clicks on your ad and visits your website, regardless of how often the listing is displayed. This makes pay-per-click advertising a results-focused advertising vehicle as compared to traditional print advertisements. With a traditional advertisement in a print magazine, you are paying to be included in the publication regardless of the results the ad produces. With pay-per-click advertising, your ad can show up on the first page of Google all day long and you will not pay a dime unless someone actually clicks on your ad.

About 25 percent of searchers will click on the paid search results if they consider the ad relevant to what they are searching for. In essence, it's a prequalifier of leads at a reasonable cost.

Your ranking in the paid search results can be improved and optimized by focusing on the following three tactics:

- **Increasing your bid amount.** The amount you are willing to pay per click determines your ranking. The more you choose to pay per click, the higher your ranking will be in the paid search results.

- **Improving the relevance of your advertisements and website.** Google wants to make sure the most relevant ads appear at the top of the search results. The more relevant your ads (and the corresponding landing pages on your website) are based on the search terms, the higher your ranking will be in the paid search results.

- **Increasing your budget.** The more you choose to invest in pay-per-click advertising, the better chance you will have of ads being consistently displayed. Using research tools like the Google AdWords Keyword Planner (adwords.google.com), you will be able to determine the approximate budget you will need for pay-per-click. Budgets can be managed on a daily basis, and they are very flexible. You can start a pay-per-click campaign with a $50 budget just to see what kind of results you can produce. I have clients who spend more than $25,000 per month on pay-per-click ads because they can tie the campaign to leads and sales they are generating from PPC.

Where search engine optimization takes months to start seeing results, pay-per-click advertising takes minutes. Your ads can start attracting targeted traffic immediately, but your campaign will require attentive management to ensure you are receiving the highest return on your pay-per-click advertising investment.

Get inside customers' heads through keyword research

The first and most important step in search engine marketing and pay-per-click advertising is to get inside the heads of your customers and uncover the keyword phrases they use when thinking about your company's products or services. If you do not perform this step properly, there is no way your campaigns will be successful.

When choosing the best keyword phrases, it is critical to choose phrases that are not only relevant to your business, but also ones that are searched most often by your target customers. The best keywords have:

- **Strong relevance to your company and website.** Niche terms related to your products or services that your website has content to support.

- **Reasonably high search volume.** Terms your most likely customers are searching on a regular basis.

- **Relatively low competition.** Terms with a relatively low number of companies competing in the search results.

There is an art and a science to the keyword research process. The art of the process focuses on brainstorming about the phrases you think your customers are searching. The science part of the process will tell you the estimated search volume by phrase, based on recent search history. Research services can help you determine this. The following steps will help you leverage this process to identify the best keyword phrases for your company.

1. Brainstorm potential keyword phrases. Begin your keyword research with the art of the process and brainstorm phrases you think customers use when searching for your products and services.

Get all your customer-facing team members involved and consider the following questions:

- What problems are our customers trying to solve?

- What terms or phrases do they use to describe their needs or problems?

- What terms or phrases do they use to describe the solutions we provide?

- How would we describe our products and services to a beginner in our industry?

- What do customers do with our products (e.g., applications, etc.)?

- What terms do industry magazines and industry analysts use to describe our products and services?

- What 10 phrases do we associate most with our company?

- What 10 phrases do we associate most with our products and services?

To assist your brainstorming process, you can leverage a number of online services that allow you to peek at what keyword phrases your competitors are focusing on with search engine marketing. Using SpyFu's free search (spyfu.com), you will be able to learn their approximate pay-per-click budget, best paid keywords, top organic keywords and other useful information.

2. Compare your brainstorming list to actual search volume. After completing the brainstorming exercise detailed above, you will have a seed list of keyword phrase candidates. Next, turn to the science of keyword research to determine how frequently people search these terms.

Keyword research tools that aggregate and estimate search volume are available to take the guesswork out of the research process. These tools will reveal the keyword phrases on your list that are frequently used by your customers, as well as the terms that are rarely used. These tools can help you expand your list by showing variations, qualifiers and alternative spellings that are also searched in high volume.

The following resources are examples that can be used for this process:

- Moz Keyword Difficulty – moz.com/tools/keyword-difficulty

- Wordtracker – wordtracker.com

- Keyword Discovery – keyworddiscovery.com

- Google AdWords Keyword Planner – adwords.google.com

Moz Keyword Discovery, Wordtracker and Keyword Discovery require a fee for the full service, but they may offer a free trial. Google AdWords' Keyword Planner tool is free to use, but you need to have a Google account to access it.

3. Prioritize your keyword list. At this stage you will know the most popular phrases by search volume, but you should not focus on popularity alone. You must also focus your efforts on popular phrases that are most relevant for your website's content and product offering. Review your keyword list and assign a priority for each keyword phrase, using the following grading scale:

- **Grade A – Top Priority:** This group of keyword phrases is very relevant to your website's content and has a high search volume and relatively low competition.

- **Grade B – Medium Priority:** This group of keyword phrases is very relevant to your website's content and has a moderate search volume or moderate competition.

- **Grade C – Low Priority:** This group of keyword phrases is very relevant to your website's content and has a moderate search volume, but it is not a desirable term to use on your website or has too much competition.

Grade A and Grade B keyword phrases are good candidates for your organic search engine optimization and pay-per-click advertising efforts. Your Grade C terms are not good candidates for organic search engine optimization but may work well for pay-per-click advertising. When optimizing your website for organic search traffic, begin with your most popular Grade A terms and work down the list.

For organic search engine optimization, focus on 30 to 50 Grade A and B phrases at a time. I recommend limiting yourself to 30 to 50 phrases because there are so many things you need to do to optimize your website. Don't spread your efforts too thin. Achieve a top ranking for your top 30 to 50 phrases, then move on to the next set of phrases, always driving more targeted traffic with each initiative. For pay-per-click advertising, it is relatively easy for you to focus on an extensive list of phrases without harming your campaign.

4. Optimize your website for organic search. Once you have uncovered your most important keywords, make sure your website's content is optimized to take advantage of them. Begin with your website copy. Make sure it effectively markets your company while using your important keyword phrases in a relevant fashion. If you do not have creative writers in-house, you can contract with many talented and affordable freelance writers on websites like Upwork (upwork.com) or Guru (guru.com), or you can hire a professional marketing copywriter to create your content. After the copy is optimized, your Web team should focus on optimizing your website coding – the HTML "under the hood" or behind the pages of your website that search engines see when they crawl your website. The optimization process includes planning, writing and coding.

5. Create a keyword plan for your website. After ranking your phrases by search volume, try to get a handle on your chances for search engine optimization success. Most likely there are millions of pages competing for the searcher's attention for a given keyword phrase. If the phrase is very competitive, you may be fighting a long, uphill battle to get on the first page.

Begin by creating a keyword plan for your search engine optimization campaign.

Assign keywords to the most appropriate pages. Review all of the pages on your website and determine the best page for each of your keyword phrases. If an ideal page does not exist, create one. Be sure to begin this process with your Grade A phrases and then move down the list.

Focus on no more than one or two related keyword phrases per page. There are only so many phrases you can work into one Web page. Ideally, you should focus on one phrase per page with each phrase assigned to a unique page on your website.

6. Write compelling, keyword-rich copy. Keyword-rich copy is critical to SEO success. Unfortunately, a lot of Web copy is poorly written because the people placed in charge of copywriting do not understand how to write for search engine success. There are a number of successful strategies for creating compelling, search engine-friendly copy for your website.

Use the keyword phrase throughout the entire page in a natural way. Your keyword phrases need to be used throughout the entire page. Preferably, every page should have about 250 to 300 words of copy, and your keyword phrase should be used 5 percent of the time – or five times for every 100 words of copy. Do not use the phrase over and over in an unnatural way. If you do, your website ranking will suffer.

Write for people, not machines. Don't write for Google at the expense of your prospects and customers. Create customer-focused copy that addresses the needs of your customers, provides a solution to their problems and is easy to read and understand. As mentioned above, it is important for you to work your keyword phrases into your copy in a natural way.

Optimize each page's headline to stress your keyword phrase. For each Web page you are optimizing, include the keyword phrase in the page's headline or title. It is more effective if you use the keyword phrase in the front of your title, rather than the end. For example, if the keyword phrase is "search engine marketing," it is better for the title to be "Search Engine Marketing: 7 Steps to Success" rather than "7 Steps to Search Engine Marketing Success."

Help Customers Find You

Be descriptive. Since you need to use your keyword phrases often, be as descriptive as possible when crafting your website copy. Avoid using generic words that do not tell your customers and prospects anything. Replace these generic terms with keyword-rich descriptive terms. For example, if you are optimizing for the phrase "bandsaw accessories," don't say "our products" when you can say "our bandsaw accessories."

Avoid excessive repetition of keyword phrases. I'm saying this again because I know it's tempting. Make sure you do not repeat the keyword phrase too many times on a Web page in an unnatural way. Not only is this a red flag for Google, it will not read well to your target audience.

Leverage different forms of your important keywords. Search engines treat different forms of words differently. Remember to use plurals, past tense (e.g., -ed) and action (e.g., -ing) forms where it makes sense.

Use bold, italics and underlines. When you emphasize a word with italics, underlines or bold, search engines assume that it is an important keyword on the page. Use this to your advantage to identify to Google the important keywords for the page. However, make sure that you only use these formatting tags on keywords or you will confuse the search engines and weaken the effect.

Link between pages. Whenever possible and practical, link to other pages from within your content and use keyword phrases for the target page when possible. Avoid using generic "click here" links.

Code your website for SEO success

Warning! If you are a non-technical person, this is the only part of the book where I need to be technical. Bear with me. I don't expect you to physically program any of these coding tips, but I want you to know what you should communicate to your Webmaster. If you are not already doing this, I recommend that you meet regularly with your tech team to discuss your online marketing goals and results. Sometimes, coders are too deep in the details and need to be reminded of the big picture to focus their efforts.

In addition to copy, your website must be optimized "under the hood" and programmed to adhere to current SEO coding best practices. To do this effectively, your Web team should have SEO masters on board to make sure you are leveraging current SEO best practices. If it doesn't, you can hire a third-party SEO expert from Upwork (upwork.com) or Guru (guru.com) to direct programming efforts. There is an art and science to this SEO coding process, and the science side can fill a book. Here are some important coding elements your technical people should focus on.

Make sure your website is "crawlable" to ensure all content gets indexed. To be found online, all pages on your website must be fully indexed by the top search engines Google and Bing (Yahoo is powered by the Bing search results). Search engines send out programs called "spiders" to crawl your website and record and categorize its content. You must make sure your website is crawlable or it will not be included in the organic results. Use clean HTML that complies with W3C guidelines and avoid dated Web development tactics like Flash-only designs or using frames. Offer accessible navigation that works for both humans and machines. Finally, include a sitemap to provide search engines with a road map to crawl through your website.

Include relevant keywords in your page <title> tags. The title tag – visible in the tab of your Web browser – is one of the most important components of an optimized Web page. Search engines consider page titles very important when evaluating page content, and it is used as the blue clickable link people will see in the search results. Title tags must be written to include the most important phrases for the page, as well as the name of your company, so it will appear compelling to the searcher and they will know what website they will be visiting. Also, keep your title tags under 60 characters including spaces. Finally, each page of your website should have a unique and relevant title tag that focuses on the unique content on the page.

Create descriptive <meta> description tags. The meta description tag is very important, since Google feeds this information into the search results below the clickable link. Craft your meta descriptions for each page as a compelling call to action. Include your most important keywords for the page, and keep them below 150 characters including spaces. Each page of your website should have a unique and relevant meta description tag.

Create useful <meta> keywords tags. The keywords meta tag has been exploited over the years by site owners stuffing it with every keyword phrase under the sun. As a result, it is largely ignored these days by Google and other search engines. Still, it may have some minor impact, so use it only to list the keyword phrase being focused on for each page.

Leverage heading tags in your pages. Search engines consider heading tags – <h1> – more important than normal text. Use heading tags on every page to highlight the most important keywords and the headline for each page.

Use targeted keywords in directory and file names. Just as you can name folders and file names on your computer to describe their contents, you can name directories and file names on your website to describe their contents. Search engines will look at directory names and file names when reviewing the content of a Web page to determine the keyword focus. Where it makes sense, use your most important keyword phrases in these names.

Use relevant keywords in <alt> tags for images. Search engines cannot read text included in images. However, every image can have an <alt> tag with a brief description that can be read and indexed by search engines. Only include relevant keywords that are important for the page and relevant for the image. Resist the urge to stuff your <alt> tags with too many keywords.

Create a robots.txt file. A robots.txt file tells search engines what you allow or don't allow them to add to their indexes. You can learn how to create this file at www.robotstxt.org. Add your sitemap location to the robots.txt to assist with the indexing of your website. Your robots.txt file should be uploaded to the root directory of your server.

Create an XML sitemap. To search engines, an XML sitemap is like a road map for your entire website. You can build a quick sitemap for your website using products like XML Sitemaps Generator (www.xml-site-maps.com). Upload your sitemap to the root directory of your server and then tell Google and Bing where it is located (e.g., example.com/sitemap.xml). A quick way to do this is with your robots.txt file. Also, update your sitemap.xml file each time you add pages to your website.

Set up a Google Webmaster Tools account. Google allows you to set up a Webmaster Tools account, which provides you with detailed reports about your website's visibility on its search engine. You will be able to see how Google crawls and indexes your site and learn about specific problems with accessing it. In addition, you will be able to share your sitemap.xml file, as well as tell Google how you would like the URLs, or Web addresses, it indexes to appear.

Avoid "black hat" techniques. Black hat techniques are schemes designed to fool Google to get higher search rankings. Google and the other search engines know all of these tricks and if you're caught you can kiss your ranking goodbye.

Good news! The technical part of this book is over! Onward and upward!

Earn inbound links to your website

Link building involves earning quality links to your website from other websites that are frequented by your customers and prospects and that are important in your industry. The more quality inbound links you earn, the more popular your website is in the eyes of Google and other engines. These links can have a dramatically positive effect on your search ranking.

Don't confuse this with outbound links (links from your website to other third-party websites). Outbound links can have a negative impact on your search ranking if they are misused.

Link building is the most impactful – and most neglected – SEO strategy. Recently, I talked to a company that learned this the hard way. They completed a sizable investment in a new website with a great design that was optimized for a top search engine position. However, they couldn't earn a ranking higher than their competitor who had a very poor website with an old, outdated design. After reviewing their situation, I determined that link popularity was the reason. Although the competitor's website was poorly designed, it had thousands of natural inbound links to a number of articles posted on its website. The company I was advising had fewer than 100 inbound links that were not from reputable websites.

I like to use the "fill the bucket" metaphor when describing link building. Think of your website as a bucket and each inbound link is a stream of water into your bucket. We want to fill your website bucket as high as possible. Each outbound link is like a leak in your bucket. You need to have many more quality inbound links than outbound links on your website.

By consistently applying the following link-building strategies, you will dramatically impact your ranking on Google and boost your online popularity.

Assess and improve your current inbound links. Are you making the most of your current links? Do you even know how many inbound links you have? If your answer is no to either of these questions, this is the best place to start your link-building efforts. Take advantage of Moz's Open Site Explorer (opensiteexplorer.org) to find a list of sites and pages that already link to you. Then make a list of sites that should have links to you but do not, including trade associations, customers, vendors, suppliers, online magazines and other business partners or industry resources. Make a thoughtful, personalized request to the owner of each of these sites and respectfully ask them to add your link.

Fix link-free references to your company online. If your company has been around a while, you may have many references to your company online without a clickable link back to your site. This is low-hanging fruit for link building. Perform a Google search for your company's name with quotation marks around the name (e.g., "SVM E-Marketing Solutions") and visit each page. If there is not a clickable link back to your site, reach out to the website owner and ask them to add the link. Don't forget to search for online references to your company's logo. Perform a Google Image search for your logo by searching "your company name + logo" and visit the pages in the results. This strategy will make the most of your current online exposure.

Create link-worthy content. One of the best ways to attract scores of inbound links is to make your website's content link-worthy. Websites with compelling and targeted content will earn links from quality third-party websites. This is another area where your content marketing efforts will pay dividends. Pack your website with great blog posts, articles, videos, guides and other content. Continually update your website with new content each month. Over time, you will see your inbound links, search ranking and search traffic continue to grow.

Share content on social networking sites. Social media marketing executed properly can be an effective link-building strategy. Tap into your content marketing arsenal once again and start sharing content on social networks. Post status updates featuring your great content to your company's Facebook page, Twitter feed, LinkedIn profile and Google+ profile. Include a compelling, brief abstract with a link back to your website for more. Not only will you gain a link from your social network properties, but if your fans, followers and connections start sharing your content, you will pick up many more inbound links to your website.

Guest post on legitimate industry websites. If you have expertise to share, there are a number of legitimate websites that are looking for content from experts like you. Look for websites of industry publications, associations and popular blogs and make an offer to write content for them. At the end of your article or blog post, put a short "About the Author" section with a link to your website. As long as you focus on legitimate industry websites that people actually use and your content is compelling, you will gain a valuable link with each posting.

Make the most of your business relationships. Most likely, the vendors, suppliers and dealers with whom you do business have websites. They offer a great opportunity for you to gain relevant links. Offer to provide a testimonial for their website that will include a link back to yours. Since they value their business relationship with you, they will likely agree.

Review your competitors' links. Take advantage of Open Site Explorer (opensiteexplorer.org) to find pages that link to your competitors. Also, perform a search on Google for your most important keywords. Anyone in the top 10 listings is your competitor, whether you know them or not. Chances are they each have great inbound links to achieve that ranking. This is a great way to determine what sites you should be targeting for your proactive link building efforts.

Avoid link-building mistakes. Almost as important as following the best practices for link building, avoid the worst pitfalls. Don't load up on reciprocal links. Unfortunately, trading links with other sites will have minimal impact on your link building efforts. Don't buy links from link farms, sites that do nothing more than list links to other websites. Google will penalize your site if they find you on these sites. Don't spam sites requesting links. It does not work and often causes more problems by tainting your online image.

Run a results-focused paid search campaign

Everything I have talked about so far will help you build your organic search ranking and traffic. Now let's switch gears and set our sights on paid search marketing opportunities. Paid search is an advertising tool and it's important to remember the difference between marketing and advertising. Marketing is the process of attracting new customers and advertising is a tool you can use during the marketing process. There are many reasons why you should include pay-per-click advertising in your marketing mix.

- **Results are immediate.** Unlike organic search engine optimization, which can take three months or more to see results, pay-per-click can begin driving traffic within minutes of launching your campaign.

- **You only pay when someone visits your website.** Unlike traditional advertising where you pay for exposure regardless of the results, with PPC you only pay when someone clicks on your ad and visits your website, providing a compelling pay-for-performance model of advertising.

- **You can reach a targeted, motivated audience.** Your ads will only display for people that are actively searching for your company's products and capabilities. In addition, you can focus your ads to show up only in front of searchers that reside within the territory you do business, as well as restrict the days/times your ads are displayed.

- **25 percent of people are attracted to paid search ads.** While not as large an audience as organic search, a significant portion of your target audience takes advantage of paid search ads.

- **Pay-per-click is inexpensive and flexible.** With pay-per-click advertising, you can start with a budget as low as $50 to test your results. You can spend as much or as little as you wish, and you can change any aspect of your campaign almost instantly. In my experience, you can expect to pay $0.50 to $5 per click, depending on the competitiveness of the keyword phrase.

- **Pay-per-click is extremely measurable.** Leveraging PPC analytics, you will be able to measure and optimize your campaign to increase your leads and sales while lowering your PPC ad investment.

The key to pay-per-click advertising is to make sure you are running a results-focused campaign that tracks your return on investment. I like to think of it more as a financial model than an advertising model. You are paying for specific visits to your website, and you want to make sure you are getting a sizable return on that investment.

Google AdWords (adwords.google.com) is by far the most popular pay-per-click advertising platform. As mentioned earlier, Google dominates business-to-business searches with a 90 percent market share. If you are just getting started with pay-per-click advertising, I recommend you focus your efforts exclusively on Google AdWords. There are a number of strategies that will help you manage a results-focused pay-per-click campaign.

Choose your paid search campaign target

One of the best features of pay-per-click advertising is how targeted it can be. You have tremendous control over where your ads are viewed, including where the visitor is located and the websites your ad displays on, as well as the devices that can be used to view your ad. Specifically, your AdWords campaign can be targeted in the following ways:

- **Geographic location.** Google allows you to set a specific geographic target for displaying your ads. This can help ensure your ads are only showing up in front of your most likely customers. For example, if you are a distributor serving southern California, you can set up your pay-per-click campaign to only show up in southern California. When I perform a search for your products from New Jersey, I will not see your ads.

- **Ad network.** When setting up your AdWords campaign, you can designate the websites you want your ads to show up on. You can show your ads on the Google Search Network, including Google.com and sites that partner with Google search, such as AOL. You also have the opportunity to show your ads on Google's Display Network, which includes third-party websites, online publications and blogs that partner with Google to display AdWords ads. If you are new to AdWords, I recommend you focus primarily on Google's Search Network to produce greater results. On the Search Network, your ads appear in front of motivated prospects who are actively searching for what you have to offer. On the Display Network, the mindset of the person is more passive and they will have little motivation to click.

- **Device.** By default, your AdWords ads will appear on all devices, but you can alter this setting at the campaign level. Specifically, you can target your ads to desktop and laptop computers, to smartphones with full browsers like iPhones or Android devices, or to tablet devices. If you select tablets or mobile devices, you have additional options to fine-tune your targeting, such as specific carriers or networks.

- **Day and time.** Some companies run AdWords campaigns just to get the phone to ring, but that only makes sense if someone is there to answer the phone. You can modify this setting at the campaign level to designate the specific days and times of day you want your ads to be displayed.

Select the best keyword phrases for AdWords

The keyword research you learned earlier in this chapter will be invaluable for your AdWords pay-per-click campaign. However, the way you use and deploy these keywords is very different from your organic SEO campaign. Since you are paying for each ad click, you want to make sure your ads are showing for targeted, niche phrases that only your most likely customers will be searching.

Begin by understanding keyword match options. Leveraging the appropriate match types can often make or break a pay-per-click campaign. Match types help control the keyword phrases that trigger your ads to display. Generally, Google offers the following match options:

- **Broad match:** Broad match is the most liberal match type and will show your PPC ad if a search term contains your keyword terms in any order and with other search terms. Your PPC ads may also show for singular or plural forms, synonyms and other relevant variations. Broad-match keywords are useful when you are not familiar with searching patterns and want to make sure you show up for all relevant searches, but it can deliver too many mishits.

- **Broad match modifier:** Broad match modifier allows you to gain greater control over when your ads are displayed with broad match. Add a plus sign (+) as a modifier to your broad match keywords if you want your ads to display when someone searches for close variants of your keywords in any order. Close variants include singular and plural forms, misspellings, abbreviations and acronyms. Broad match modifier excludes synonyms or related searches.

- **Phrase match:** Phrase match adds even more control as to when your ads are displayed. Putting the keyword phrase in quotes converts it to phrase match, meaning the characters between the quotes must appear exactly in the actual search.

- **Exact match:** Exact match is the most effective way to exclude searches you don't want to attract. By placing [brackets] around your keyword phrase, your ads will appear only when someone searches for your exact keyword without any other terms in the search query.

- **Negative match:** Negative match allows you to filter out irrelevant searches and prevent unwanted clicks. Your PPC ads won't show if a search query contains the keyword term that you define with a minus sign (-) prefix.

The following table provides examples of how each of these match options will influence when your ads are displayed.

Match type	Example	Ads may show for	Ads will not show for
Broad Match	work boots	buy work boots best boots for work work boot laces snow boots work shoes	No limits
Broad Match Modifier	+work+boots	work boots buy work boots best boots for work	snow boots work shoes
Phrase Match	"work boots"	black work boots tan work boots buy work boots	boots for work snow boots work shoes
Exact Match	[work boots]	work boots	black work boots tan work boots buy work boots
Negative Match	"work boots" - tan	black work boots buy work boots	tan work boots

In addition to filtering the types of keyword matches to prevent unwanted – and potentially costly – clicks, Google's Keyword Planner within the AdWords system will help you to get a handle on the AdWords opportunity by estimating traffic and costs by keyword. Enter the phrases on your keyword list into this tool, and it will tell you the estimated daily impressions of your ads and the number of clicks you can expect, as well as an estimate of the daily cost and cost per click.

After you have identified your best keyword phrases, organize them into logical Ad Groups. Focus on a handful of tightly focused phrases that are related to a common theme. Advertisements are created at the Ad Group level, but keyword phrases are what actually trigger the ads. To ensure the most relevant ad is displayed, the keyword phrases in an Ad Group must relate to that ad. The more specific your Ad Group structure, the better your ads will perform.

Create compelling pay-per-click ads

With so many options competing for a searcher's attention, your pay-per-click ads really need to stand out on the first page. Unlike traditional advertisements, paid search ads impose strict character limits. You'll notice when you write your first ad that there is little room to work with, so take care to make sure each element is as clear and concise as possible.

Understand the "haiku" of pay-per-click ads. As with the classic Japanese poetic form, pay-per-click ad text needs to fit within certain parameters.

- **Headline:** The headline is limited to 25 characters, including spaces. To make the most of this concise space, use simple words and include the keyword phrase wherever possible.

- **Body copy:** The body copy is limited to two lines of up to 35 characters each for a total of 70 characters. In this brief space, you need to convince the searcher that your offering best serves their needs.

- **Display URL:** The display URL can be up to 35 characters. Google's policy states that your display URL must match your landing page URL, so create a short landing page URL that includes your keyword phrase.

Headline ⟶	eRoom - Free Trial
Body Copy ⟶	Online project management made simple. Try it free for 15 days!
Display URL ⟶	www.eRoomHosting.com

Get inside the heads of your customers. Your pay-per-click ads are the carrot you can dangle in front of customers to get them from Google to your website. When writing your ads, make sure you understand your customers' needs and motivations. Include a compelling offer in the ad text to entice your customers to take action.

Add sitelinks for your top performing ads. Ads that appear at the very top of search results are allowed to spice up their listing by presenting additional sitelinks. They allow you to display up to six additional links in the ad to take people to other pages on your website. With those six additional links, you can feature multiple products or services and include additional offers to draw people to your website.

Send people to a relevant and unique landing page. With each pay-per-click ad, you can designate a specific landing page in which to direct traffic. Don't make the mistake of sending paid search traffic to your home page; that's probably not the most relevant place to send most searchers. To make the most of that paid visit, send visitors directly to the most relevant product page within your website. If the best page does not exist, create a new one specifically for this paid search campaign. This page should be designed to speak to the needs and motivations of the searcher, provide the solutions they are seeking and make it easy for the searcher to take action.

Tie your bidding strategies to results

Make sure you let results drive your bidding strategies. Don't fall short like so many companies do and focus on the amount you're paying for each click. Think cost per lead and cost per sale instead of just cost per click.

You'll notice that I called them "bidding strategies." That's intentional. Everything in this process should be thought out, monitored and adapted as necessary. In other words, it needs to be approached strategically.

Set up Conversion Tracking. Conversion Tracking is a tool offered by Google AdWords that shows you what happens after a customer clicks on your ads – if they purchased a product, filled out a lead generation form, signed up for your newsletter, etc. By tracking conversions in AdWords, you will know the ads, keywords and campaigns that are producing business-building results. You also will be able to track the cost per conversion in addition to the cost per click. Cost-per-conversion data is crucial to ensure that you are only bidding on phrases that convert and that your bids are not more than what you consider to be a reasonable new customer acquisition cost.

Don't always shoot for the #1 position. Unless you want to show that you are the top brand in the category, it's usually not smart to bid for the top spot. It can be very expensive to get there. Often a lower-positioned ad will produce a better return on investment because the cost per click will be lower.

Bid on relevant keyword phrases. Resist the urge to bid on keyword phrases based on popularity alone. Instead, focus on the most relevant keyword phrases for your company and products. With pay-per-click advertising, popular phrases are often expensive. Your money can be better spent by focusing on relevant niche phrases that are directly in line with your offering and used by your target audience

Test, test and test again. With pay-per-click advertising, you can measure everything. This information can be invaluable for fine-tuning your paid search campaign to improve results. Test different bidding strategies. Test different ad copy. Test different offers in your calls to action. Test different landing page designs. There is always room for improvement, and every little improvement will increase your paid search ROI.

That wasn't so bad, was it?

Okay, I realize that, for the old dogs, this chapter has been fairly technical. But in teaching you some new clicks, it's inevitable that you'll face a few that seem overwhelming. If you found your eyes glazing over from some of the details here, consider this: Your competition is very likely wide awake, sipping some coffee and tweaking their SEO and AdWords campaigns.

If nothing else, I've provided you with a detailed outline for overseeing the operations of your advertising and marketing departments, tech team and copywriters. Remember: This isn't an exercise in technical mumbo-jumbo. By mastering this stuff, your company is more likely to create great relationships with prospects and customers, and to become more sustainably profitable.

Chapter 8
Nurture Relationships with Social Media

If you follow the latest trends in online marketing – and maybe even if you don't – you have probably heard plenty of buzz about social media. Marketing professionals throughout the world are praising social media sites like Facebook, Twitter, YouTube and LinkedIn as the answer to all of our marketing prayers.

What is social media and should you jump on the marketing bandwagon? In this chapter, I will separate the hype from the helpful in social media marketing so you can figure out if your business should dive in and integrate social media into your marketing mix. If you do take the plunge, I will provide you with strategies and tactics you can use to produce results.

What is social media marketing?
Social media marketing is the latest addition to the online marketing mix. It involves leveraging social networking websites to share relevant and interesting content with your network of fans, followers and connections. Social media marketing campaigns typically focus on creating compelling content that attracts attention and encourages readers to share it across their social networks. From a relationship-building perspective, it offers a unique opportunity to connect with others with minimal cost and in a manner in which many of your customers and prospects will be comfortable.

There is a lot of confusion about social media marketing and its various components, so it is important to define a number of terms:

- **Social media:** Social media is a broad term used to describe information created in text, image, audio and video forms that can be easily shared and distributed in online social networks.

- **Social networks:** Social networks are online platforms, such as Facebook, Twitter, YouTube and LinkedIn that allow people to share social media with their followers, friends and connections.

- **Social media marketing:** Social media marketing is the process of engaging social media on social networks and other websites to nurture customer relationships.

A simple way to understand social media marketing is to think of it as public relations. However, instead of pitching the media, you are pitching your peers – without the appearance of pitching them. As detailed in the diagram below, by sharing useful and relevant content with members of your network, your message can achieve a tremendous reach: Your network shares your content with members of their networks, who share it with members of their networks, who share it with members of their networks, and so on, and so on, and so on.

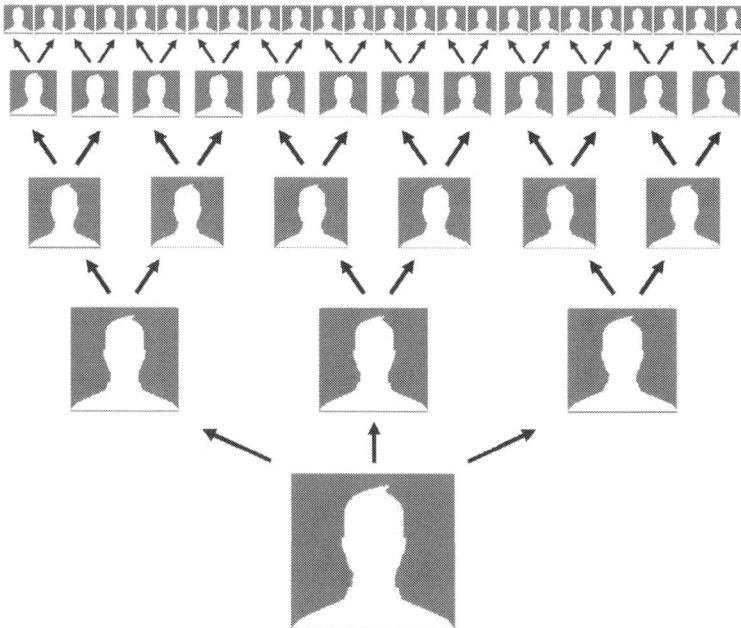

As a manufacturer or distributor, you may think social media marketing is not for your business. There was a time when I would have agreed with you, but a number of significant changes in the online world have changed my mind. Most significant is that the line between social media marketing and search engine marketing is becoming increasingly blurred. Google now tracks each website's social media activity to help determine its search ranking. Websites with content that is widely shared on social networks earn the coveted first-page position. If you think social media marketing is a waste of time, it's time to change your opinion.

How to get started with social media marketing

Are you already an active participant in the social media community? If so, you are prepared to start leveraging it as a marketing tool. If you are not, it's time to get your feet wet. You need to have a good understanding of the social media landscape before you can harness its marketing potential. To get started, follow this three-step process:

1. **Join the community.** Identify a number of social networks and social media websites and join the communities. This is the best way for you to get an understanding of the lay of the land. Set up a profile for yourself on LinkedIn, Twitter, Facebook and other social networking sites described in the next section.

2. **Listen to the conversation.** Once you set up your profiles, start listening to the discussion. Browse online communities related to your industry and frequented by your customers. Read posts by experts in your industry. You can do this manually by visiting each social networking site. You can also automate the process using software like HootSuite (hootsuite.com) that updates you about the people, topics and discussions **you care about.**

3. **Participate and create.** After listening for a while, you will have an understanding of who the players are, what they are saying, the topics and information that the community finds important and how your competitors are involved. Now it is time for you to start participating and creating. Reply to topics with your opinions, add value to the discussion and share your ideas. After participating

in the discussions of others, start your own by creating valuable content the community will appreciate and respond to.

By following this three-step process, you will be a social media pro in no time. Now it's time to learn about where you should be spending your time and resources.

The social networking landscape

There are so many social networks out there that it can seem overwhelming. Many companies fail to get started with social media marketing because they are confused about which networks to get involved with. Generally, there are two broad categories of social networks: relationship social networks and content sharing social networks.

1. Relationship social networks

Relationship social networks are based on the type of relationship that you have with your community. The major relationship social networks include:

- **LinkedIn:** The social network for business relationships. LinkedIn provides a platform for connecting with colleagues and sharing business happenings and ideas.

- **Twitter:** The social network for broadcasting. Twitter is a microblogging platform that allows people to broadcast 140-character tweets and connects followers to people and information they find interesting.

- **Facebook:** The social network for friends and family, but also for certain business applications. Facebook provides a platform for sharing ideas, happenings, photos, videos and other information.

- **Google+:** The social network for circles of connections. Much like Facebook, Google+ provides a platform for sharing; however, connections can be grouped into circles for personal, targeted sharing. While Facebook allows you to apply filters, Google+ makes it easier.

2. Content-sharing social networks
Content-sharing social networks are based on the type of content that you are sharing with your community. The most popular content-sharing social networks include:

- **YouTube:** The social network for videos. YouTube allows you to publish and view videos.

- **SlideShare:** The social network for slides. SlideShare provides a platform for publishing and viewing slide presentations.

- **Pinterest:** The social network for pictures and links. Pinterest is a content-sharing service that allows people to collect and share images from websites and to easily link back to the source of those items.

- **Scribd:** The social network for documents. Scribd provides a platform for sharing whitepapers and guides.

How to market on relationship social networks
Now that you have an understanding of social networking, you need to understand how to put the relationship social networks to work. Each network needs a unique approach to be effectively used as a marketing tool.

1. LinkedIn
LinkedIn (linkedin.com) is the most professional of the major relationship social networking websites. Since it is largely focused on business-to-business connections, LinkedIn should play a big part in your social media marketing strategy. At its most basic level, LinkedIn allows you to set up a personal profile and connect with other professionals you know or want to know. You will receive status updates on a regular basis as your connections update their profiles. In addition, you can set up a LinkedIn profile for your company to allow people to follow your company's updates.

One of the cool features of LinkedIn is the "six degrees of separation" approach that allows you to easily see how you are connected to someone via others. You may be surprised to see how closely you connect to your prospects or customers – and how connected they are to others, including your competition.

Think of your LinkedIn profile as an interactive resume on steroids. In addition to listing information about your work experience and education, LinkedIn allows you to enhance your profile with interactive capabilities that showcase your expertise:

- **Status Updates:** One of the best ways to keep your connections informed about your happenings is by posting status updates, brief statements that you feel your connections will find useful. They can include links to related content on your website or third-party websites. To appear active in the LinkedIn community, post useful and actionable status updates on a regular basis.

- **Presentations:** If you post presentations and other content to SlideShare (slideshare.net), you can display them in your LinkedIn profile.

- **Recommendations:** LinkedIn makes it easy for you to request recommendations from your connections. A collection of glowing recommendations that underscore your expertise and experience will significantly enhance your profile.

- **Projects:** Showcase any notable projects you've worked on, including a link to project details and a list of the team members you worked with.

- **Skills & expertise:** List your skills and expertise on your profile to help others understand your strengths and improve your ability to be found. Connections will be able to endorse your skills by providing their seal of approval.

- **Publications:** Showcase any publications that you have written or publications that have featured your work.

- **Volunteering & causes:** List organizations you support and causes you care about outside of work.

- **Patents, courses, test scores, certifications, languages and awards:** All of your most important accomplishments can be presented for your connections to see.

In addition to your personal LinkedIn profile, you can create a company page to tell your company's story, showcase your products and services, share updates with followers and recruit new employees. Your company page can feature:

- **Banner image:** The banner image is the first thing people will see when they visit your company page. Design one that reflects your company's brand and the image you want to portray.

- **Products & services:** Feature your products and services including rich descriptions, images, feature lists, YouTube videos and Web links.

- **Status Updates:** Status updates on your LinkedIn company page can feature content from your website with links back to the detail. For a fee, you can also promote your updates throughout the LinkedIn community through sponsored updates. The key is to post updates regularly.

- **Career opportunities:** For a fee, you can post open positions to recruit new employees.

LinkedIn community features

In addition to your personal profile and company page, LinkedIn provides a number of community features that allow you to communicate and collaborate with other LinkedIn users, including:

- **Groups:** LinkedIn groups help you stay informed and keep in touch with people who share your interests. You can create your own LinkedIn groups or join any number of groups that focus on your area of interest or expertise. Expand your circle of influence by participating in discussions in various LinkedIn groups.

- **Influencers:** LinkedIn influencers enables you to connect with well-respected thought leaders in many walks of life. Influencers like Tony Robbins, Guy Kawasaki and Richard Branson, as well as many lesser-known experts, contribute original content in the form of blog posts. You can comment on their posts and share them as status updates on your personal LinkedIn profile.

Tips for using LinkedIn as a marketing tool

LinkedIn is a valuable tool that can help you grow your business and catapult your career. The following tips will help you use this resource to produce results:

- **Brand your LinkedIn address:** When you create a personal LinkedIn profile, it will create a LinkedIn Web address that will appear like a collection of odd letters. You can customize this address to create a branded LinkedIn address with your name. My LinkedIn address is linkedin.com/in/bobdestefano.

- **Become an expert:** Post educational status updates and actively participate in LinkedIn group discussions to establish yourself as an expert and thought leader.

- **Warm-call sales prospects:** If you're in sales, you can use LinkedIn as a warm calling tool. If there is a prospect you want to reach, find them on LinkedIn and see how closely you are connected to them. If you have an active list of LinkedIn connections, you are most likely only two or three connections away from the prospect. Use LinkedIn's introduction feature to ask one of your connections for an introduction.

- **Find rock star employees:** Successful business people are always looking to find valuable employees that will ensure their future success. LinkedIn's recruiting tool can be much more effective than traditional recruiting websites since you can target applicants based on experience and expertise.

- **Keep your connections current:** Whenever you meet someone, connect with them on LinkedIn. It's a great way to expand your influence and keep connections up to speed on your accomplishments. For best results, be sure to personalize your introduction message.

2. Twitter

Twitter (twitter.com) is a real-time microblogging network that connects you to people and information that you find interesting. With Twitter you can share 140 character tweets with your followers and other interested parties. In addition, you can choose to follow other individuals you have interest in. When you follow someone on Twitter, their tweets appear on your Twitter feed. A major difference between Twitter and other social networking websites is that you do not need other people's permission before you can follow them, as long as their accounts are public.

On Twitter, you commonly post original tweets to your followers. Ideally, this information is content your followers will find useful and interesting. In addition to posting original tweets, you can retweet (or RT for short) a tweet of someone you follow. This is one of the highest honors one can earn on Twitter and it is one of the best ways to increase your following.

Your Twitter profile is pretty simple. There aren't many pieces of information that you can manage or manipulate, so it is important for you to use each of them strategically:

- **Full name:** Enter your first and last name. Use your real name if you are tweeting for yourself or your company name if you are tweeting on behalf of your company. To create a real and lasting relationship on Twitter, be open and honest about your identity.

- **Handle:** Create a username for your Twitter account (e.g., @bobdestefano) that will be used in your personal URL (e.g., twitter.com/bobdestefano). People need to remember and recognize your name to find you, so use your own name or your company name.

- **Bio:** Create a short bio that will let people know who you are, what your expertise is and what information you have to share. Make sure your bio is compelling and understandable (with no jargon) to increase the likelihood that people will follow you. But also make sure it's concise. Your bio is limited to 160 characters, including spaces.

- **Photo:** Choose a profile picture that will help others identify you easily and help them understand who you are. Use your personal photo if you are a spokesman for your company. If not, a company logo can work well if you are tweeting on behalf of your company.

- **Header image:** The header image is a horizontal bar that appears behind your photo and bio. When designing a header image, choose a design that reflects your brand while complementing the photo.

- **Web address:** Include your Web address so people will know where they can find you. Leave off the "http://" and the "www" if you can, as in bobdestefano.com, to keep your address as short as possible.

- **Location:** Add a location (e.g., Red Bank, NJ) so that people know where you are based.

- **Background design:** Your Twitter page can have a unique and personalized background design. Use this design as a branding tool and to include other contact information.

Twitter community features

While it appears to be a very simple service on the surface, Twitter provides a number of community features that allow you to communicate and collaborate with other users:

- **Tweet:** A tweet is a 140-character or less text message that you share with your Twitter followers. While it began as simply text-based content, Twitter now allows sharing of photo and video content.

- **Retweets:** A retweet (or RT) is a type of message posted on Twitter that shares information previously tweeted by another user. When you come across interesting content shared by a Twitter user, retweet it to your followers, making sure to include RT and their name (e.g., @bobdestefano) in the message. If people regularly retweet your posts, you are doing the Twitter thing right!

- **Hashtags:** Hashtags allow you to label and categorize tweets. A hashtag is a word or phrase preceded by the "#" symbol. For example, if you are tweeting about "social media marketing," you can use the hashtags #socialmedia and #smm to label your tweet. Clicking on a hashtagged word in any message shows you all other tweets in that category. But don't be a hashtag spammer; limit your hashtags to three or less per tweet.

- **Direct messages:** A direct message is a private message sent via Twitter to one of your followers. When you send a direct message, it is private; The rest of your followers will not see it. Send direct messages when they make sense, but don't abuse them by bothering people.

- **Lists:** Lists allow you to organize the people you're following on Twitter. Again, if people add you to their lists you are doing the Twitter thing right!

- **Favorites:** When users like a tweet, they can flag it as a favorite. Favorites are generally used to let the original poster know that you liked their tweet or to save the tweet to read later.

Tips for using Twitter as a marketing tool. Twitter can serve as a valuable marketing and customer service tool if you are committed and continually share content that people will want to read. But take care to use the tool effectively.

Tweet value, not nonsense. This should go without saying, but I'm going to say it anyway: No one cares what you just ate for lunch. No one cares that you just took four Advil tablets for your bad back. It's ridiculous how much nonsensical crap is flowing through Twitter. Don't contribute to the nonsense. Tweet content your followers will find helpful and actionable, such as:

- **Your educational content:** Post a link to new blog posts, videos and articles you've published to your website.

- **Other people's content:** Post a link to someone else's educational content that you found to be valuable. You can also retweet another person's interesting tweet.

- **Events you are attending:** Post a link to the webinar or conference that you are attending. Be sure to include the event's hashtag.

- **Converse with people:** Chat with Twitter users by including their handle (e.g., @bobdestefano) in the tweet. This will help them notice your tweet so they can respond.

- **Something interesting you observed:** If you noticed something interesting that your followers would find valuable, post a tweet with a picture.

Become a friendly resource. To effectively market yourself or your company on Twitter, establish yourself as a friendly, go-to resource for your area of expertise. Don't blatantly tweet about your products or services. Tweet about your knowledge and expertise as they relate to your products or services.

Build a strong following. You need to offer a compelling reason for people to follow you. The best way to do so is to tweet valuable content. Next, follow interesting and successful Twitter users with a strong following. If these people find you interesting, they'll follow you and retweet your content. Also, use hashtags in your tweets related to your content or expertise (I use #b2bmarketing a lot). This will allow you to easily get your tweets in front of like-minded individuals.

Brand your Twitter look. You can choose from several available background designs from Twitter, or you can upload your own. A custom background that reflects your brand and includes additional contact information can be an effective way to brand your profile. Create a compelling header that complements your brand. Also, upload a Twitter avatar that is an attractive photo of your smiling face or your company logo.

Obey Twitter etiquette: Twitter etiquette runs the gamut. Don't be offended if someone doesn't return your follow. Keep the boring tweets to yourself. Don't send direct messages to people you do not know. Don't be misleading. Don't be afraid to be personal, but don't be overly personal. The list goes on and on. Think of Twitter (and most social media sites) as a form of online public relations. If you don't want your clients to read it in the newspaper, don't tweet it on Twitter.

Of all of the social networking sites, Twitter requires the most work. If you neglect your account, your follower count will drop quickly. Remember the virtual pet key chains from the 1990s? If you didn't care for them regularly, they got sick and died. The same thing will happen to your Twitter account. It needs consistent TLC, but in return, it will pay dividends.

3. Facebook
Facebook (facebook.com) is by far the largest social networking website, with more than 1 billion registered users. Its user base is so large that if Facebook was a country, it would rank among the largest in the world. For the most part, Facebook is a place for friends and family, providing a platform to connect (or reconnect) and share ideas, happenings, photos, videos and other information. It also offers widgets and apps that you can integrate into your Facebook page to make it more engaging.

As a business, you can use Facebook as a marketing tool. By creating a Facebook page for your business, you create a public-facing Facebook destination that your customers can access easily without you having to approve them. You can use this page as an outpost for your website's content.

Facebook provides a number of ways to customize your business page to service your marketing needs. The essential elements of your Facebook business page include:

- **Name:** The name for your page should be the name of your company or name of your product.

- **Cover photo:** Choose a cover photo that represents your brand and showcases your product or service. It's the first thing people will see when they visit your page. It's important to use an eye-catching cover photo that is relevant to your business. You may want to change the image every few months or so to give your business page a fresh look.

- **Profile picture:** Choose a logo or another image that people associate with your business to use as a profile picture.

- **Description:** Your business page description should clearly explain who your company is, the purpose of your page and what customers can expect to get from it.

- **Custom tabs:** You can also add an unlimited amount of tabs to your Facebook page, though only four will be visible on the main page. Think strategically about the content you want in these slots (e.g., photos, groups, events, etc.).

- **Posts:** Posts are the main content on your Facebook page and should be updated regularly. Use posts to start conversations with visitors, offer educational content from your website, share useful content from third-party websites, share special offers or promotions and post photos or videos.

Facebook's community features for business pages

Facebook is a great platform for sharing your multimedia content with your customers and prospects to attract them to your website. Specifically, the community features of Facebook pages include:

- **Sharing content:** Facebook is all about sharing ideas, thoughts, photos, videos, etc. Your business page should be all about sharing useful information related to your area of expertise. Think of your

Facebook business page as an outpost for your valuable website content.

- **Like:** Like is a critically important concept on your Facebook business page. You need to be "liked" to be successful. The success of your Facebook business page is judged by how many people like it. Likewise, everything you post on your business page is judged by how many people like it. When people like your content, their friends will become aware of it as well.

- **Comments:** In addition to liking your content, people can post comments regarding your content. Try to be active and interact with your fans when they comment on your content.

Tips for using Facebook as a marketing tool

Your Facebook business page can serve as a valuable marketing tool that allows you to bring your content directly to your customers. These tips can help you get the most marketing value out of your Facebook page:

- **Use SEO to help your page get noticed:** Unlike personal pages, your Facebook business page is freely accessible to anyone – that includes Google! Use your important keyword phrases throughout your content.

- **Consider advertising on Facebook:** Similar to Google AdWords, Facebook offers a flexible, self-service advertising vehicle to help your ads appear in front of your most likely customers. If it makes sense for your company, test it out and see if it drives new business.

- **Create custom tabs for your business:** Facebook allows you to create custom tabs to enhance your page and help market your business. You can use Facebook Markup Language (FBML), which is very similar to HTML, to create compelling content and features.

- **Integrate your social media offerings:** Facebook Apps make it easy for you to integrate your blog, Twitter profile, LinkedIn profile and other social media content. Take advantage of these features to make sure you are cross-promoting all of your social media content.

- **Offer Facebook deals:** Deals allow you to reward customers with special offers without the need to provide them with a coupon. This self-service marketing tool allows you to easily create a deal, specify a start and end date and designate the number of claims you will allow.

4. Google+

Google+ (plus.google.com) is the newest entrant into the social networking landscape. You may be thinking: "Why in the world would we need another social network?" I thought the same thing after it launched, but quickly changed my mind once I discovered the innovative way Google+ structured its network.

I have always had a problem with how social networking made me treat my relationships. If I wanted to keep business relationships separate from friend and family relationships, I had to use different social networking sites: LinkedIn for business and Facebook for friends and family. And I don't even like how they treat my relationships within each of these social networking sites. Is my relationship with my employees the same as my relationship with my accountant? No! Is my relationship with my college roommate the same as my relationship with my mother? No! Yet on LinkedIn, Facebook and Twitter, they treat all my connections, friends and followers the same. For the most part, everybody sees everything.

Google+ has solved my social networking problem with its circles feature. Google+ circles are collections of connections that you can drag and drop into logical groups that reflect your existing social circles in the real world. You can create separate circles for family, work colleagues, college friends, customers, association members, bowling team, board of directors, etc. Then, as you share your updates, you can pick the appropriate circle(s) that can view your updates. In addition, you can quickly click between the news streams of your different circles. Finally, your Google+ profile can be customized by circle, so you can hide elements of your profile from certain circles. Note: Other social networking sites are retrofitting their services to offer similar functionality to mimic circle functionality (e.g., Facebook Lists).

Google+ also offers companies the ability to set up business pages. I strongly recommend that you set one up because it is believed that your Google+ activity can positively impact your search ranking. Your Google+ business page includes:

- **Category:** Select a category (e.g., local business, product or brand, company, etc.), but do so carefully. Your category selection will influence your placement and presentation. For example, if you are a local distributor serving a fixed geographic area, pick "local business" so you can bubble up in Google's localized search results.

- **Name and website address:** Add basic information to identify your company, including company name and website address.

- **Cover photo:** Choose a cover photo that represents your product, company or brand, one that can promote and enhance your business.

- **Story:** Write a short and compelling tagline, as well as a lengthier description that will tell your company's story. Describe who you are, what you do and who you do it for.

- **Links:** Add links to your company's website, including deep links to featured content on your website.

- **Photos and videos:** Post interesting company photos organized into albums, as well as videos you posted to YouTube.

- **Posts:** Posts are the primary content on your Google+ business page. Update your posts regularly with interesting content your customers will find valuable.

Google+'s community features for business pages
Participation in Google+ is becoming critical for online marketing suc-

cess. In addition to the ability to share content and communicate with your customers, your Google+ activity can influence your search ranking. Google+ offers a number of community features including:

- **Sharing content:** As with Facebook, Google+ can serve as an outpost for your website content. Continually create and post relevant content to your website and share it on your Google+ page.

- **+1:** This is the Google+ version of the Facebook like. You want to accumulate as many +1's as possible because it is a strong measure of the quality of your content.

- **Circles:** As mentioned earlier, circles are a way of organizing your Google+ connections. They allow you to share targeted content with targeted groups of people.

- **Hangouts:** Google+ Hangouts are video chats that can be conducted one-to-one or in groups. You can set up a hangout for group meetings, online events or customer presentations.

Tips for using Google+ as a marketing tool

Your Google+ business page can serve as a marketing tool and can have a positive impact on your search ranking. These tips can help you get the most out of Google+:

- **Optimize your About section for SEO.** When writing your tagline and introduction, use your most important keyword phrases. Include links to the most important pages on your website. These enhancements will boost your website's SEO, while providing more opportunities for you to get in front of searchers.

- **Segment your circles.** Figure out the best way to categorize your circles. Think about the content you plan on sharing and organize your circles based on their interest in specific content.

- **Add Google's +1 button to your website.** It is widely believed among SEO practitioners that +1 activity influences search rankings. The more +1 likes your content receives, the higher that content will be presented in the search results.

How to market on content-sharing social networks
Content-sharing social networks allow you to publish a specific type of social media (i.e., whitepapers, presentations, videos, images, etc.) and allow viewers to comment and share with their networks. There are several sites you should consider for your social media marketing mix.

1. YouTube
YouTube (youtube.com) is the most popular video-sharing social media site and offers you an opportunity to promote brand awareness, position yourself as a thought leader, demonstrate your products and enhance your SEO efforts. YouTube videos, if optimized properly, can be displayed in the Google search results for your most important keyword phrases, so it is important to make sure you are optimizing them with SEO in mind.

To make the most of your YouTube presence, follow these tips:

- **Create a branded YouTube Channel.** YouTube allows you to create a branded outpost to host your videos by changing the color scheme or uploading a custom background. Try to visually align your YouTube channel and website.

- **Produce short educational videos.** Think of useful educational content that your customers will find valuable, and start filming. Produce a video blog post of you speaking about an interesting topic. Film a product demonstration or best practice. The videos do not need to be professionally produced; a simple digital camera will do. Keep your videos under 10 minutes in length. The shorter, the better, as long as you are getting your main points across.

- **Use annotations in videos.** After uploading your video, YouTube allows you to add annotations to your videos. Annotations let you add interactive commentary to your videos. You can use them to add background information about the video, create stories with multiple possibilities (viewers click to choose the next scene) or link to related YouTube videos, channels or search results from within a video.

- **Use captions in videos.** Similar to annotations, YouTube's caption feature allows you to make your videos more accessible and understandable. Adding captions and subtitles make your videos easier for people to follow along with if they don't have speakers, speak a different language or are hard of hearing.

- **Optimize your videos for SEO.** Use relevant keyword phrases in the video title and description. Tag your video with targeted keyword phrases to make it easier to find on YouTube. Finally include a link to your website at the top of the description. Make sure you use the "http://" in the link (as in http://bobdestefano.com) to make it clickable.

Note: YouTube is not the only video site available. Other video sites to consider include Vimeo (vimeo.com), Dailymotion (dailymotion.com) and Metacafe (metacafe.com).

2. SlideShare

Think of SlideShare (slideshare.com) as the YouTube of PowerPoint presentations. It allows marketers to share presentations and documents. Members of the SlideShare community can then add comments, download content and share with their networks. SlideShare is one of the best ways to get your presentation slides on the Web to reach a wider audience. Your SlideShare content can be easily indexed by search engines. Also, it is easy to syndicate your SlideShare content on your blog, as well as your relationship social networking sites like LinkedIn.

To make the most of your SlideShare presence, I encourage you to follow these tips:

- **Create a branded SlideShare profile.** When you set up a SlideShare account you can brand certain elements of your profile. Make the most of these elements to make your profile stand out.

- **Create compelling presentations.** Think of useful educational content that your customers will find valuable and fire up PowerPoint or Keynote. Create presentations detailing how-to tips or best practices. Feature an educational customer case study detailing how they benefited from your product or service. Highlight industry trends and how your customers should modify their businesses to remain competitive.

- **Put a call to action in the last slide.** Give your viewers a logical next step to take advantage of your company and learn more. Include contact information, a link to your website and, most importantly, a compelling offer that they can't refuse.

- **Optimize your presentations for SEO.** When you put together your presentations and upload them to SlideShare, use relevant keyword phrases in the title and summary. In addition, make sure you tag your presentations with relevant keyword phrases so that users can find your content when searching on SlideShare.

Note: Other slide sharing sites to consider include SlideCorner (slidecorner.com) and SlideServe (slideserve.com).

3. Pinterest

Pinterest (pinterest.com) is a virtual scrapbook that allows people to create and manage categorized image collections for their interests and hobbies. People can browse other people's pinboards for images they like and repin them to their own pinboard. Also, like other social networks, people can like other people's images. Businesses are using Pinterest to drive traffic and links to their website by showcasing product photos, infographics, whitepaper covers and other content.

To gain a marketing advantage with Pinterest, follow these tips:

- **Create a branded Pinterest profile.** Create a branded outpost to showcase your images. Customize it with your company logo and information about your business.

- **Own your niche.** Make the goal of your Pinterest pinboard to own your niche. Aim to provide the best content available that focuses on your expertise.

- **Post pictures of your products in action.** Instead of posting static pictures of your products, post pictures of customers using products. Compelling product images like these are more engaging.

- **Generate leads by showcasing content.** Create landing pages on your website with short opt-in forms for your downloadable content (e.g., how-to guides, whitepapers, case studies, etc.). Include an attractive image as the cover image of the document on the landing page. Then, pin this image onto your Pinterest pinboard, including a brief description of the image and a call to action that asks people to visit your website to access the content.

- **Engage with other Pinterest users.** Participate in the Pinterest community by liking and repinning related content of others. By engaging with others, they will engage back and share your content with a broader set of people.

Other image sharing sites to consider include Flickr (flickr.com) and Picasa (picasa.google.com).

4. Scribd

Now it's time to market your whitepapers and guides. Scribd (scribd.com) is a social media site for sharing documents, allowing readers to print, comment and share with their networks. Scribd is a great resource for sharing the PDF documents in your content marketing arsenal with your online audience. Your Scribd content can be fully indexed by Google, allowing you more opportunities for your content to bubble up in the search rankings.

To make the most of your Scribd presence, follow these tips:

- **Create a branded Scribd profile.** As you set up your Scribd profile, punch up your bio to include descriptive information about your expertise and experience to help your profile stand out.

- **Create compelling documents.** Think of useful educational content that your customers will find valuable and start writing. Create 8- to 15-page whitepapers that demonstrate thought leadership on issues that are important to your customers. In addition, create lengthier e-books that present complex information in a compelling and entertaining way.

- **Include a call to action on the last page.** After your readers consume your great content, they may be hungry for more. Direct them to a resource center on your website that provides additional articles, videos and whitepapers on the same subject. Also, include your contact information to make it easy to get in touch with you.

- **Optimize your content for SEO.** When you create your content and publish to Scribd, make it SEO-friendly by using relevant keyword phrases in the title and summary. In addition, make sure you tag your documents with relevant keyword phrases so that users can find your content when searching on Scribd.

Note: Other document-sharing sites to consider include Issuu (issuu. com) and Calameo (calameo.com).

It's in the area of social media that the old dogs are least likely to have their tails wagging. But this is also perhaps your greatest untapped potential in terms of marketing online due to the personalization, information-sharing and relationship-building capabilities it offers. Neglect it at your peril. Embrace it and tie it into your other online marketing efforts, and you will find your reach and your profitability soar.

Chapter 9
Nurture Relationships with Email Marketing

As a marketer, your goal is to get prospects and customers to buy your products – instead of those of your competitors – and keep them coming back for more. To make this happen, you need a cost-effective way to communicate that builds your relationship with them and transforms them into valuable, loyal customers. That's where email marketing fits in.

Email marketing has a bad reputation because too many companies use it as a prospecting tool. As a result, most people don't look at their email inbox to decide what to read, but rather to decide what to delete.

Email is not a prospecting tool; it is a relationship-nurturing tool. Email works effectively when it is used to nurture relationships with people you already know by sending information they want to receive. Unfortunately, most manufacturers and distributors are clueless about how to produce business-building results with email.

What is Email Marketing?
Email marketing is an important component of an integrated online marketing strategy that leverages permission-based electronic communications to nurture relationships with customers and prospects, generate leads and sales, and enhance customer retention. Email marketing offers a number of advantages over other marketing methods.

- **Email is cost-effective.** Creation, production and delivery costs for email are much lower than traditional direct mail. And while postage costs are continually rising, email delivery costs are declining.

- **Email can be personalized.** With targeted email, you can speak directly to each customer and prospect, addressing their unique needs and desires. Email allows you to easily segment lists based on interests and personalize content within each message.

- **Email provides timely feedback on results.** Emails are delivered almost instantaneously and 80 percent of messages are opened within two days of delivery, according to studies. You'll know quickly if your email campaign is a success.

- **Email can help you get more value out of your website.** You have invested a lot of time and money in your website. Email can help you boost your return on this investment by driving prospects and customers back to your website on a regular basis.

- **Email provides a strong return on investment.** When planned and executed effectively, email will inspire your customers and prospects to take action and respond to your offers. When coupled with its cost-effectiveness, email produces a substantial ROI.

Email marketing is all about relevance and respect. If you embrace this simple principle and make it the core of your email marketing strategy, you will be successful. Unfortunately, too many companies ignore (or don't understand) this principle, leading to the problem of unsolicited and unwanted email messages. To avoid having your emails perceived as spam, make sure you have a good understanding of what email marketing should be – and what it shouldn't be.

Email marketing <u>should</u> be:	Email marketing <u>shouldn't</u> be:
Permission-based	Unsolicited
Personalized	Broadcasted to everyone
Customer-centric	Company-centric
Relevant	Deceptive
Predictable	Haphazard
Respectful of privacy	Exploitative

Setup an email campaign management system

Don't use your personal email account for email broadcasts. An email marketing campaign management system will help you automate the entire process of building your lists, designing and delivering compelling messages and measuring the success of your campaigns. You don't need any special technical skills to use most of these systems. Most have tools that will guide you through the process of creating and distributing your emails, which makes the process very easy.

At the lower end of the price range, email campaign management systems like Constant Contact (www.constantcontact.com) and MailChimp (www.mailchimp.com) provide a great set of base-level capabilities at a very affordable price. At the higher end of the price range, email campaign management systems like ExactTarget (www.exacttarget.com) provide more advanced capabilities such as dynamic content presentation, automated trigger emails, advanced reporting and more. Or, if you want to outsource the entire process, a capable online marketing agency can manage the email marketing process for you, providing a turnkey solution for your entire email marketing campaign.

Build an email list online and offline

The key to an effective email campaign lies in a notion known as "permission marketing." Your email campaign should build goodwill with your customers and prospects, not annoy them. Therefore, you need to obtain their permission before adding them to your email marketing mailing list. I strongly recommend you focus the majority of your efforts on building your own in-house list, rather than purchasing or renting a list from a publisher or list broker.

Build your in-house email list online

Begin by building your email list online. Your website is a great place to grow your email subscriber base. Leverage the following tips to make the most of this process:

- **Offer your email sign-up on every page on your website.** Your email sign-up should be a consistent call to action offered on every page of your website. It's the best way to build your house list.

- **Add a "subscribe to our email list" checkbox on every form on your website.** Every lead generation form or inquiry form on your website should include a checkbox allowing people to easily sign up to your email list. But be clear about what they're signing up for.

- **Make sure your email sign-up form is short and simple.** Don't scare away subscribers by asking for too much information right away. The more information you ask for, the fewer people will complete the form. I recommend you just ask for their name and email address. You can build out more demographic information later.

- **Show that you are trustworthy.** Make sure a link with your privacy policy is clearly presented on every sign-up form. Make it clear to subscribers that you will not misuse their personal contact information. And let me repeat, make sure you're clear about what they are signing up for.

- **Offer an incentive at sign-up.** You will get more subscribers if you also offer an incentive, such as a whitepaper, "how-to" guide or discounts on future purchases, in exchange for their information.

- **Allow people to review your educational e-newsletter, if you have one, prior to sign-up.** An effective way to entice people to subscribe to a regular offering is to let them sample the goods. On your email sign-up form, provide a link to prior issues so they can see how valuable your e-newsletter is. (I'll discuss creating the newsletter later in this chapter.)

- **Include a "subscribe to our email newsletter" call to action in your email signature.** Add a brief statement to your personal email signature that describes the benefits of your e-newsletter, such as "Subscribe to our e-newsletter for tips on how to grow your business."

- **Show appreciation and say thank you.** Send a welcome email thanking new subscribers immediately after they sign up. Include a link to your e-newsletter archive for their convenience.

- **Encourage subscribers to "forward to a friend."** Your customers are probably friends with your best prospects. Make it easy for subscribers to help you build your list.

Build your in-house email list offline

Often your offline interactions with customers and prospects are a great opportunity to build your email list. Talking with them face-to-face can provide an extra level of trust that you can't get via the computer.

- **Ask your customers for their email addresses and permission.** Whether it's done over the phone or in person, ask salespeople and customer service people to tell all of your current customers about your email newsletter and ask permission to add them to your list. If you are a distributor with a retail location, have an email sign-up list on the counter where customers pay.

- **Promote your email list in all printed marketing materials.** Whether you're producing a brochure, letter or direct mail post-card, always include a line asking the recipient to sign up for your email newsletter.

- **Tout your email newsletter on invoices and packing slips.** Any transactional communications you have with customers are opportunities to grow your list.

- **Promote your email newsletter on product registration and warranty cards.** Have a check box to let customers sign up to receive your email newsletter.

- **Collect email addresses at trade shows and other events.** As people visit your booth, let them know about the great educational resources you offer. Just ask for their permission and business card.

- **Send postcards to customers encouraging them to subscribe.** If you have postal mailing addresses for customers but not email addresses, send a postcard with an invitation to subscribe to your email newsletter.

Segment your list to tailor content for targeted groups

If your company serves a variety of distinct industries or business types, consider segmenting your list into separate groups. This will allow you to send targeted, relevant messages to each of these distinct audiences. You can do this manually by creating groups within your email subscriber database, or you can let your customers do it for you. By providing a variety of segmentation options on your email subscription form, your subscribers will segment themselves during the sign-up process.

How to effectively use rented lists

So far in this section, I've focused mainly on ways to build your house email list. This is because I want you to focus most of your email list-building efforts on building your own house list. But what about purchasing or renting a third-party email list from a publisher or list broker? While not recommended as your primary list building method, third-party email lists can work if you adhere to the following best practices:

- **Rent lists, never buy them.** If someone sells you a list that you can use as often as you wish, it is not permission-based. However, if a publisher or third-party rents you a list that you can use one time through the publisher's broadcast email system, it is most likely permission-based.

- **Drive them to your website so they can join your list.** The primary goal of your rented list email campaign should be to drive recipients to your website so they can opt into your email list by signing themselves up. Then, you will own these subscribers' email address to use for your future campaigns.

Create an educational email newsletter

Email marketing with a monthly e-newsletter offers you an opportunity to build an ongoing, interactive dialogue with your customers and prospects on a measurable, cost-efficient basis. Not only can an e-newsletter demonstrate value to your customers, but it can also change your customers' perception of your business. By sending timely articles that solve current business problems, you show your customers that you understand them and their needs. This repeatedly reinforces their importance to you and builds their trust in your company.

If any of the following apply to your company, you should seriously consider producing an email newsletter:

- You rely on repeat customers.

- Your prospects are not ready to buy right now.

- You can benefit from referral business.

- You have valuable information to share.

- You want your customers to view you as a partner.

The big challenge in conducting a successful email newsletter campaign is generating content that will motivate prospects and customers to open, read and respond. Email newsletters that simply provide a recap of the latest products and news from your company will be read only by your most loyal customers. To reach out and influence all potential buyers, you need to provide useful, objective information that can help your prospects and customers do a better job.

Once you get in the habit of providing valuable information that fits your company's business, you will find it easy to unobtrusively slip in a sales message that will be likely to catch your prospects and customers in a very receptive frame of mind.

Find an expert and an editor

Your company should have a great writer and a great editor for your email newsletter. Your writer is the expert responsible for creating compelling, customer-focused articles and content for your email newsletter. Your editor is responsible for reviewing and editing content, managing production and distribution, and ensuring the voice of your e-newsletter is maintained issue after issue.

Both of these people may already exist within your company, so how do you choose the right people?

Is your company president a talented writer? His or her insights into hot topics or emerging trends in your industry can serve as the expert voice for your e-newsletter. Or, perhaps you have another thought leader in your company that can create e-newsletter content. Even if this expert is not a talented writer, he or she can work with a talented copywriter to craft and polish a compelling e-newsletter article.

The editor is responsible for your email newsletter campaign as a product. He or she is responsible for reviewing and editing e-newsletter articles, ensuring that the voice of your company rings clear in each issue. In addition, this person is responsible for managing the production and distribution of your e-newsletter. Finally, your editor should monitor the results of each e-newsletter to measure the success and gain actionable insights to influence the success of future email newsletters. This role can be filled by a member of your team or an online marketing agency.

Write relevant, customer-focused articles

Your email newsletter is not for you – it's for your customers. Focus less on your company and more on the issues and ideas your customers are interested in. I like articles that focus on how-to tips, best practices and actionable strategies. To help get you started, the following are examples of useful e-newsletter content:

- **Problems and solutions.** Identify common problems that your readers might face and provide ideas on how to solve them.

- **Technological developments.** Inform your readers on how to take advantage of recent technological developments to improve their operations and be more effective.

- **Lists and statistics.** Provide actionable lists and statistics with titles like "Seven Steps to _____," or "Top Five Ways to _____," or "The Top Ten Tips for _____."

- **Industry news and trends.** Write about new developments in your industry that are relevant to your readers. Make sure to highlight why they are important for your readers' businesses.

- **Case studies.** Write case studies of how others have improved their operations. Make sure to include details that readers can learn from and success measures so your readers can gauge the results achieved from these actions.

Many companies pack way too much content in each issue of their email newsletter. Focus on one idea per issue and resist the urge to explain your entire field of expertise in each e-newsletter. You'll have more content to choose from for your next issue, and your readers will find your newsletter easier to read.

In addition, your articles need to be short and to the point. The best e-newsletter articles are between 500 and 750 words of text. Also, with email newsletters, you have about five seconds to convince someone your email is worth reading before they delete it. Make your e-newsletters easy to scan by breaking up the text in your articles into manageable chunks. Use bullet points and bolded headers to make it easy for your readers to scan and absorb your message.

Make a call to action

Even though the focus of your email newsletter is to educate prospects and customers, this is a great opportunity to present them with relevant offers to generate leads and sales or encourage repeat website visits.

Remember the e-newsletter 80-20 rule. Email newsletters should be 80 percent educational and 20 percent promotional. The majority of the email newsletter content is useful educational information, while the sidebar is presenting your readers with an attractive offer that is relevant to the article content.

Make sure your offer is relevant. I know I mentioned relevance in the previous paragraph, but it is important to repeat this idea again. Your offer must be relevant on a number of levels to be effective. It should be relevant to the reader's interests and to the focus of your article content. This offer could be for a related product or for a related content item on your website.

Email customers targeted promotions

When executed effectively, promotional email marketing is an excellent way to promote new products and encourage repeat purchases. According to a study by Convince and Convert,[1] 44 percent of email recipients make at least one purchase per year based on a promotional email and those customers spend 138 percent more than people that do not receive email offers. So if you are not sending out promotional emails, it's time to start.

Unfortunately, most manufacturers and distributors don't know how to effectively approach promotional email marketing, with many of them just emailing a PDF of their weekly flier. That approach is not going to work! To be effective with promotional email, follow these proven best practices:

1. Create customer-focused promotions

Promotional email marketing campaigns too often center around products a company wants to sell instead of products customers want to buy. This is a recipe for lackluster email marketing results. To be successful with promotional email, think carefully about your customers' needs and create offers that will cause them to "Act now!"

Know your customers and offer something they value. The key to successful promotional offers is to understand what drives your customers and to offer them something that adds value to the purchase. Examples could include "buy one, get one free," limited time discounts or a gift (e.g., $50 Starbucks gift card) for purchasing a certain dollar amount. Brainstorm offer ideas with your salespeople to determine what type of promotional offers would be perceived as most valuable to your customers.

Focus on a single customized offer targeting specific customer segments. Resist the urge to promote many products in your email messages. The most effective promotional messages are simple to understand

---

1   Nelson, Amanda, "25 Mind Blowing Email Marketing Stats," Salesforce.com, July 12, 2013, https://www.salesforce.com/blog/2013/07/email-marketing-stats.html.

and focused on a single offer targeting specific customer segments. According to a MailChimp study, "Effects of List Segmentation on Email Marketing Stats,"[2] emailing customized promotional messages to specific customer segments increases open rates by 14 percent and click-through rates by 59 percent, as compared to general broadcast messages.

Mine your sales data to create personalized promotions. Your customers' past purchases can help you uncover effective offer ideas. By mining your sales data, you can create personalized offers to buy again, buy more or try a complementary product. For example, you can search your sales data to find a segment of customers who purchased a drill within the last 30 days. Then, you can create a promotional email for this segment of customers with a discount on drill bits. This strategy works very well for cross-selling related products and expanding the breadth of products each customer purchases from you.

Send perfectly timed promotions for products that expire. If there are certain products that you know your customers will need to reorder at a certain time, create timed, personalized promotions to make it easy for them to reorder. For years, I have been buying coffee for my office from a small online coffee reseller. The primary reason they get my continued business is because they happen to know exactly when I'm running low on coffee and send me an email with my personalized order allowing me to purchase with one click.

Have a firm deadline and/or limited quantities available. Effective promotional offers create a sense of urgency. You can accomplish this by setting a firm date when your offer will end. Another way to create urgency is to limit the number of offers or quantities available. People will respond faster if they know they need to be one of the first 50 people to respond.

2. Design your promotional emails for success
Even the most compelling promotional offer will fail if the email message

---

2   "Effects of List Segmentation on Email Marketing Stats," MailChimp, updated Mar. 1, 2016, http://mailchimp.com/resources/research/effects-of-list-segmentation-on-email-marketing-stats/

is not well designed. Promotional messages need to quickly catch your customer's attention, communicate the value of your offer and make it easy for them to take the next step. Promotional email design and layout is important because customers tend to scan email messages first before reading them in detail.

Choose an effective promotional email template. With email campaign management systems, such as Constant Contact, you often begin with a predesigned template that you customize with your company's branding elements. Promotional emails are very different from email newsletters, so choose an email template that presents the offer and call to action prominently.

Write compelling subject lines. The goal of the subject line is to get the recipient to open the message, not accept the offer. In fewer than 50 characters, you need to state the immediate benefit of opening your message to create a sense of urgency and importance. (For example: Ending Soon: Get up to 50 percent off.) To determine the best subject lines, many companies A/B test different subjects to small segments of their list to find the most effective one before the big blast.

Use a familiar "from" address. Most email recipients use the from line in your message to determine if they should read or delete the email. If customers are used to doing business with specific salespeople, have the from address include the salesperson's name and your company name as in: *Bob DeStefano, SVM E-Marketing Solutions*. If there is no specific contact person they normally deal with, use your company's name.

Make a clear call to action. Make it as easy as possible for the reader to take advantage of your promotion. Present bold, obvious buttons for readers to click. Make sure the button links to a page on your website where people can place an order and take advantage of the promotion. Cut down the number of steps it takes to convert your readers into purchasers.

Email marketing has been around longer than other online forms of marketing because email was popularized and in wider use before the

Web. So many old dogs are more familiar with email marketing than with other forms of online marketing – and that may not be a good thing. Email marketing has received plenty of bad press of late, and for good reason. Well-meaning people and companies have abused it to spam prospects and browbeat customers into immediate purchases they likely don't want or need. But done properly, email marketing is a fantastic tool in your overall marketing plan.

Chapter 10
Optimize Your Marketing for Mobile

We all know that smartphones have become ubiquitous in society and in the business world. All you have to do is look at people in an elevator, on a bus or train, or in a boring meeting. They are staring down and poking a little rectangular device in their hand. According to a study performed by Forbes magazine in 2010,[1] 82 percent of business executives use smartphones, a number that is probably far closer to 100 percent by now. It's clearly time to think about how you can use those little rectangular devices to grow your business.

What is mobile marketing?

Mobile marketing is an increasingly important part of your marketing strategy that allows you to communicate and engage with customers on the go through their mobile devices. Broadly, this refers to smartphones, mobile phones, wireless handheld devices such as the iPad or ultra-portable netbooks, and so forth. However, the focus for mobile marketing is usually on smartphones. Mobile marketing has largely been a B2C phenomenon, but B2B marketers are making it a priority as more people use smartphones as business tools.

How essential is mobile marketing for your company? Is it a critical issue for you to address immediately, or is it something you have some time to assess and address? The best way to answer this question is by checking out your Web analytics reports. Web analytics is software that tracks visitor behavior on your website. If you're using a contemporary Web analytics package, such as Google Analytics, you will be able to gain great insight into mobile use of your website.

If you are using Google Analytics, log in and look at the mobile usage section within the "Audience" tab. This section will provide you with

---

1 "The Untethered Executive: Business Information in the Age of Mobility," Forbes, 2010, http://images.forbes.com/forbesinsights/StudyPDFs/The_Untethered_Executive.pdf

a wealth of information about mobile usage of your site, including the number of people accessing your site from smartphone and tablet devices. You will also get detailed information about the device brand, service provider, operating system, screen resolution and the locations from which visits originate. This information will help you uncover your mobile opportunity.

If your mobile traffic is under 5 percent, you have some time to address mobile marketing. However, if mobile traffic is 5 percent or higher, it's time to get serious about marketing on the small screen.

Optimize your website for the small screen

Pull out your smartphone and visit your website. If you are like most B2B companies, your site is hard to read, hard to navigate and hard to take action on from a mobile device. According to a Google study,[2] "What Users Want Most From Mobile Sites Today," your bad mobile website is not only frustrating customers, it is also tainting the way they feel about your company. More than half – 52 percent – of customers say that a bad mobile experience makes them less likely to engage with a company. In addition, 48 percent say that if a website doesn't work well on a smartphone, it makes them feel like the company doesn't care about their business. It's time to stop turning off mobile customers and to optimize your website for the small screen.

A great way to approach a mobile website is to leverage a responsive Web design. Responsive Web design enables you to build and maintain a single website that works well on all varieties of devices, including laptops, smartphones, tablets, etc. Leveraging flexible images and fluid grids, content and design layouts automatically resize to fit the screen no matter how large or small. This allows images to grow or shrink as necessary and text copy to reflow itself, providing all visitors with a consistent experience on all smartphones, tablets and desktop computers. To see an example of responsive design in action, visit SVM E-Marketing Solutions' website (svmsolutions.com) and make your Web browser

2   "What Users Want Most from Mobile Sites Today," Google, Sept. 2012, https://www.thinkwithgoogle.com/research-studies/what-users-want-most-from-mobile-sites-today.html

window larger and smaller.

While creating a responsive website is a great way to go, it is no small task. It takes a Web development team with a special skill set, a content management system that supports responsive design and a higher investment in time and money. However, this investment will pay dividends over time.

If your website is powered by a mainstream content management system, there are other alternatives. Many mainstream content management systems, such as WordPress (www.wordpress.com) or Drupal (www.drupal.com), have mobile plug-ins available that will automatically convert your content into a specialized mobile website. If your website detects that a visitor is using a mobile device, the server will automatically dish out your mobile site, as opposed to your regular website.

Finally, if you have an older, static website and are looking for a quick and easy way to create a mobile version, take advantage of mobile makeover services like DudaMobile (www.dudamobile.com). With DudaMobile, you can create a mobile website in just minutes. Just go to DudaMobile's website and type in your website URL. DudaMobile will quickly index your Web content and reformat it into a mobile format. You will be presented with an interactive version of your mobile website in just minutes, and you can easily customize the mobile site's elements as desired. It's a pretty amazing service that costs less than $10 per month. With DudaMobile and the other options discussed above, every company should have a mobile-friendly website.

Create apps to serve customers and sales reps

Apps are software applications designed to run on smartphones and tablets. Apps are what make smartphones smarter, providing advanced capabilities for people to play games, manage finances, book travel, compose music, etc. The list of app capabilities is endless. In addition to a mobile-friendly website, your company could offer specialty apps to serve your customers and improve the productivity of your sales team

A number of industrial distributors, like Grainger, have designed mobile apps to allow customers to search for products, place orders and check the status of shipping. If your company is looking to do the same, it may not be a time-consuming or expensive ordeal. Many ERP software vendors are offering app modules that make it easy for you to mobilize your business processes.

Mobile apps can also enable your sales team. Stop sending them out with bulky catalogs and brochures. Give them an iPad instead. By creating specialty apps for your salespeople, you can empower them with mobile sales kits to access product content, demonstration videos, pricing, data sheets, competitor information and customer contact information. This allows salespeople to be more nimble when they're on the road, always having instant access to information to answer customer questions.

The creation of apps could be straightforward, as in the ERP example, or it could require custom development. Also, there are many companies creating app toolkits that are tailored for specific marketing and business applications. Search the Web for a packaged solution before you create something custom for your company. In many cases you will find "there's an app for that."

Integrate QR codes into your print marketing

Have you noticed the unusual-looking square boxes that appear in magazine advertisements, postcards and other print marketing pieces? These two-dimensional bar codes are known as QR codes, which stands for quick response codes.

When scanned by smartphones, QR codes connect the offline world with the online world. As a marketer, you can add QR codes to your print ads, catalogs, business cards, brochures and other print marketing to direct prospects to a corresponding mobile landing page that contains much more information than can be presented in a print piece. This allows you to present an extended marketing message and add a new level of interactivity to your offline marketing efforts. You can easily create your own QR codes for free by taking advantage of a number of online services, including Kaywa (kaywa.com), QR Stuff (qrstuff.com) and ScanLife (scanlife.com). Just input the Web address or URL you want to direct people to and a custom QR code will be instantly created for you.

There are a number of creative ways your company can enhance your marketing with QR codes. The following examples have worked well for companies similar to yours:

- **Extend the message of your print marketing.** In most print marketing, space constraints limit your marketing message. By adding QR codes with corresponding landing pages to your brochures, catalogs, product sheets and other print marketing, you can communicate an extensive marketing message that includes interactive content.

- **Connect in-store shoppers to your website.** If you are a distributor or dealer with a retail location, enhance the in-store shopping experience by adding QR codes to product displays that direct customers to a landing page with extended product information, demonstration videos, frequently asked questions and other useful content.

- **Use QR codes to boost your social media engagement.** Instead of sending people to your website, you can use QR codes to direct people to your social networking outposts on LinkedIn, Facebook, Twitter or YouTube. You also can use services like QR Stuff (qrstuff. com) to create QR codes that will automatically like your Facebook page, post a status update on Twitter or share content on LinkedIn.

- **Connect your tradeshow booth with your website.** Strategically place QR codes in your tradeshow booth and other displays to send people to your website. They may not have time to stop and talk with you, but they can quickly scan a QR code to learn more about your products and services from your mobile website.

- **Add QR codes to products and product packaging.** QR codes can also be used for customer service purposes. Add QR codes on your products and product packaging to link customers to a page where they can access user manuals, demonstration videos, replacement part order forms and other useful information about the product.

- **Use QR codes to help build your email subscribers.** As I mentioned in the last chapter, you should always be building your email subscriber list both online and offline. Use QR codes on your print marketing to direct people to your email sign-up form to make it easy for them to subscribe.

Optimizing your online presence for mobile devices is nearly as far as an old dog can get from "back in the day." Your willingness to consider this important component of your online marketing strategy will serve you well in the months and years to come.

If you have somehow managed to avoid using a smartphone for your own personal or business use, this may be the time to bite the bullet and get one. Have a millennial show you how to use it. It may not revolutionize everything you know about business and marketing, but at the very least you can see what all the fuss is about – and how your ever-younger customers and employees interact with their world!

Chapter 11
Make Your Marketing Measurable

How will you know if your online marketing program is a success? Gone are the days when an industrial marketer could execute a campaign without tying it back to bottom-line results. As a 21st century marketer, you can no longer rely on subjective measures, gut feeling or esoteric statistics like hits. To be successful with online marketing, you need to be able to accurately measure the bottom-line impact your website and other online marketing activities are having on your business and determine the strategies that deliver the greatest return on investment.

ROI needs to be as fundamental an ingredient in marketing as it is in finance, sales, R&D or any other strategic department in your company. Each of these departments has quantifiable success measures they use to gauge their progress and success. The same idea should apply to your marketing. One of the reasons I love online marketing is that it is completely measurable. When evaluating the success of any marketing activity, you can easily track your progress by monitoring the following success measures:

- **Web traffic:** Is the marketing activity producing an increase in traffic to your website?

- **Conversions:** Are the offers and calls to action on your website converting anonymous visitors into named individuals for your marketing database?

- **Leads:** Are any of the conversions turning into qualified leads that may result in a near-term business opportunity?

- **Customers:** Are the leads you are generating turning into profitable new customers?

By tracking these success measures for each marketing activity, as well as the investment you made in each activity, you will be able to measure ROI through these success measures:

- **Customer acquisition cost:** How much money did you invest in the marketing activity to acquire each new customer? Does the average customer acquisition cost for that activity afford an acceptable profit margin?

- **Effectiveness by marketing channel:** Which marketing activity produces the highest return on investment? By carefully evaluating this measure, you will be able to cut your marketing budget while increasing your leads and sales.

Measure the success of your website

Since your website is the hub of your marketing, it is the first place you should focus when measuring your marketing results. Your website must have a Web analytics system in place to measure how well your website is working toward achieving your business goals.

For most companies, I recommend Google Analytics. It does a fantastic job of making Web statistics easy to understand and – believe it or not – the service is free. Some Web analytics packages focus too heavily on technical statistics. Google Analytics is more focused on helping you measure marketing results. These reports will show you how people found your site, what content they looked at and what calls to action enticed them to reach out or buy online. This provides you with information on the current success of your website and provides ideas for how you can enhance your campaigns to improve your results in the future.

Google Analytics reports are very easy to set up. Go to Google (analytics. google.com) and set up a free account. Google will provide you with a small block of code to put on all of your website pages. From that point forward, Google Analytics will track your valuable visitor data. Google Analytics offers a rich report set that provides great detail on the key metrics you need to monitor to ensure your online marketing campaign is a success, including:

- **Audience:** The audience reports provide insight into key information about the people who are visiting your website, including who makes up your audience (demographics, location, language, etc.), technology used to reach your website (Web browser, operating system, network, mobile device, etc.) and how engaged they were with your website (pages viewed per visit, time spent per visit, etc.).

- **Acquisition:** The acquisition reports help you understand how you are attracting visitors to your website (traffic source by channel, campaign keyword and medium), their behavior on your website after acquisition (average pages viewed per visit, visit duration, and total page views) and their conversion activity (conversion activity by transactions, revenue, goal completions, etc.).

- **Behavior:** The behavior reports help you understand how people are interacting and engaging with your content. You will learn about your most popular content, the speed of your pages, internal site search queries, engagement with interactive elements and which page elements are drawing the most clicks.

- **Conversions:** The conversions reports track the completion of important activities on your website, such as placing an order, completing a form or subscribing to an email newsletter. Each activity can be programmed as a goal to allow you to track the completion of these activities. If you have an online shopping website, you can configure e-commerce tracking to analyze online sales effectiveness.

Even if you do not intend to make changes to your website, I recommend you put Google Analytics in place immediately. You will start tracking valuable data that will come in handy in the future. You will know what's working and not working on your existing website, as well as have baseline data you can use to judge future enhancements.

Measure your search marketing success

To ensure your search engine marketing campaign is a success, you must measure your organic search engine optimization and paid search efforts to monitor performance and identify actionable strategies to improve your results. For organic SEO, begin by tracking your ranking in the search results for your most important keyword phrases. You can do this manually or take advantage of software packages like Web CEO or Advanced Web Ranking to do it for you. Then, check the acquisition section of Google Analytics to see if you are experiencing traffic gains from organic search. Finally, check Google Analytics to see if you have goal completions from organic search (e.g., request a quote form completions, online sales, whitepaper downloads, etc.).

To measure results from your paid search campaigns, enable Conversion Tracking in Google AdWords. You will be provided a bit of code to add to your online form confirmation pages. This will communicate back to Google each time you earn a conversion from paid search visitors, allowing you to track not only your cost per click but also your cost per conversion. Then, enable the AdWords hook with your Google Analytics account. This will allow you to track all site activity that occurred between the click and the conversion. Monitor your Google AdWords and your Google Analytics reports on a regular basis to track your cost per click and your cost per conversion by keyword phrase to make sure you are not bidding more than a reasonable customer acquisition cost. In addition, you should monitor the performance of your paid search ads and enhance them as necessary to boost results.

Measure your social media marketing success

According to the PricewaterhouseCoopers Manufacturing Barometer survey,[1] a majority of U.S. industrial companies have trouble measuring social media marketing ROI. I can understand their frustration. Too many companies measure social media marketing success by only counting esoteric measures such as likes and followers. Unfortunately, these measures don't go far enough to demonstrate ROI and, according

---

1   "Q3 2011 Manufacturing Barometer," PwC US, Oct. 26, 2011, http://www.barometersurveys.com/vwAllNewsByDocID/CA2BB63A33FA2BD7852578800053C44C/index.html

to research from BrandGlue,[2] more than 85 percent of people who like a Facebook business page never return to it again.

So how do you really measure social media marketing success? There are three key measures to monitor: reach, engagement and conversion.

1. Reach: How many people did you impact with your message?

The first place to start is to measure your reach, or the number of people you have impacted with your social media content. If everyone is ignoring you in the social media world, you're doing something wrong and you'll never produce results. Reach will give you a good understanding of how attractive your social media content is to your target audience. Examples of reach metrics include:

- Connections on LinkedIn

- Followers on Twitter

- Likes on your Facebook page

- Views and subscribers on your YouTube channel

- Visitors to your blog

You can measure reach by keeping track of these statistics manually. In addition, social networking sites, including LinkedIn, Facebook and Twitter, all have analytics reports you can access. Finally, take advantage of third-party services like Klout (klout.com) or Radian6 from Salesforce (salesforcemarketingcloud.com) to track your reach for you.

2. Engagement: How many people interacted with your message?

After you have an understanding of your reach, the next step is to see if anyone cared enough about your message to actually do something with it. By measuring engagement, you will have access to this vital information. To engage people with social media, create valuable content that inspires people to interact with you. If your engagement level is low, you need to take a critical look at how to improve your content. Examples of

---

2 Lasica, JD, "Tactics to stay on your fans' radar – begin with targeting their news feeds & making your updates count," SocialMedia.biz, Feb. 10, 2011, http://socialmedia.biz/2011/02/10/15-ways-to-extend-your-brand-reach-on-facebook/

engagement metrics to track include:

- Clicks on links in your social media posts

- Retweets, mentions and direct messages on Twitter

- Shares on Facebook and LinkedIn

- Comments on your Facebook, YouTube and LinkedIn posts

- Ratings on your YouTube videos

- Comments on your blog posts

Just as with reach, you can measure engagement by keeping track of these statistics manually or you can leverage third-party services to track these metrics for you.

3. Conversion: How many people took action because of your message?
Finally, it's time to measure the business-building impact of your social media marketing efforts. Conversion will tell you how many people took the next step to enter your lead generation funnel and join your marketing database. A critical best practice for social media marketing success is to use your website as the hub of your social media content, always linking back to content on your website in your social networking posts. In addition to this content, your website should offer content upsells and lead generation offers to convert anonymous visitors into named leads for your sales process. Examples of conversion metrics to track include:

- Registrations for content downloads

- Webinar registrations

- Online lead generation form completions

- Phone-in leads

- Online sales

To effectively track conversion, I recommend a number of free resources. While Twitter and Facebook offer their own proprietary conversion tracking systems, the following methodology can be used to track web-site conversions uniformly. First, integrate Google Analytics into your website to track your site activity. Next, leverage campaign tracking in Google Analytics and build trackable links for each of your social media posts. As you do this, you'll notice the links are way too long to include in your social media posts. Use a URL shortening service like Bitly (bit. ly) to shorten your links . Finally, leverage goal tracking in Google Analytics to track all of your online conversion activities (e.g., downloads, registrations, etc.). This will close the loop, allowing you to track ROI from your social media marketing campaigns.

Measure your email marketing success

One of the most appealing aspects of email marketing is the ability to measure results. That is why I always encourage marketers to use an email campaign management system like Constant Contact to run their campaigns. When using an email marketing campaign management system, you will have access to great reports that allow you to track the key metrics to measure the success of each email marketing blast. Metrics to monitor include:

- **Delivery rate** tells you whether your email is actually making its way to the intended recipient's inbox. If your delivery rate is not 90-95 percent, you probably have some bad addresses on your list.

- **Open rate** lets you know how many people opened your message. For a successful message, your open rate should exceed 30 percent of your subscribers.

- **Click-through rate** shows you the percentage of people who opened your email who clicked on any links in the message. Depending on the offer, your desired click-through rate will vary; however, a click-through rate above 10 percent is generally considered a success.

- **Forward rate** tells you the percentage of readers who forwarded your message to a friend or colleague. If you get any forwards, your message was a success.

Make Your Marketing Measurable

- **Unsubscribe rate** is the percentage of people that unsubscribed or opted out of receiving future communications. This percentage should be as close to zero as possible, but anything below 2-3 percent is fine.

Look at these statistics after each email message, and compare the statistics of each email blast to determine the content and offers that are causing your readers to respond. You can use this information to improve the engagement of future email blasts.

In addition to looking at your campaign management system statistics, look at your Web analytics reports to track activity of email visitors. These reports will tell you what Web content your email subscribers are interested in, as well as what calls to action in your messages are generating the most leads and sales. In addition, you should track which sections of your website are generating most of your new subscribers.

Measure all marketing success

Once you get a taste of online marketing measurement, you will be hooked. Soon you will want to measure results for all of your marketing, including print ads and direct mail. Marketing analytics provides you with the solution. Leveraging trackable campaign IDs and unique toll-free numbers, marketing analytics allows you to track the results of all online and offline campaigns.

Here's how it works. Each marketing activity will be assigned an online campaign ID, a unique phone number and a unique URL. A postcard, for example, will include these unique identifiers. If someone calls from the phone number on the postcard, the marketing analytics system will tie the call to the postcard. If someone visits the Web address on the postcard and fills out a form, the campaign ID allows the system to tie the form inquiry to the postcard. In addition, the phone number on the website will be dynamically generated to be the trackable phone number from the postcard. Finally, you will be able to completely close the loop to track all online form- and phone-based leads generated from all online and offline marketing campaigns.

Remember, becoming proficient in online marketing is neither a fad nor changing for change's sake. It's a vital skill as business culture and practice keep abreast of personal technologies and human habits and preferences. I didn't write this book to make you feel bad about what you don't know. I wrote it to share the awesome potential of online marketing and provide you with a basic understanding of how it works. Done poorly, it's almost worse than not doing it at all. Done well, it can be the engine that drives your company to sustainable profitability going forward. And that's a new click that any old dog can learn!

Do Something!

You made it! By reading this book, you are now equipped with a 21st Century Marketing Road Map, and you know how to effectively market to Generation Net. In addition to purchasing this book, you invested your valuable time in reading it. I am appreciative and thankful for this investment. However, for this investment to produce a return for you, I have one request before you leave: *Do something!*

It is extremely important for you to use the information you learned in this book and that you start today. Some of the ideas I've shared, like setting up Google Analytics, enhancing your website's calls to action and making better use of your home page, are fairly simple to implement. Other ideas, like putting a content marketing plan into action, search engine optimization and social media marketing, may take more time. Make a prioritized list of tasks and put them into action.

Here is my recommended course of action to get you started:

- **Put Google Analytics in place.** You can't manage what you can't measure. Begin reviewing these reports regularly.

- **Start creating valuable content.** Remember, one good idea can be used to create multiple content items.

- **Focus on your website.** Since it's the hub of your marketing, start with your website before you venture out to search campaigns and social media. Enhance your calls to action, improve your home page and make your content more customer-focused.

- **Then, turn to search.** Start a results-focused, paid search campaign as you work to boost your organic ranking.

- **Start nurturing customers with email.** Build your customer lists, put a campaign management system into place and start a customer-focused campaign.

- **Get social.** Create an outpost on each of the major social networks and get into the habit of sharing content regularly.

- **Be mobile friendly.** Set up a DudaMobile website until you can create a new website with a responsive design.

Following even this basic path will help you become an online marketing success. There's no question that online marketing is current and future reality. Why not get started right away, and on the right foot?

Good luck and happy marketing!

Resources

Many useful Websites and resources were mentioned in this book. Below please find a complete list for your reference.

Online Brand Monitoring Resources

Google Alerts	https://www.google.com/alerts
Social Mention	http://www.socialmention.com
Hootsuite	https://hootsuite.com
Klout	https://klout.com
Twitter Search	https://twitter.com/search-advanced
Viralheat	https://www.viralheat.com
Sprout Social	http://sproutsocial.com

Freelancer Sourcing:

Upwork	http://upwork.com
Guru	http://guru.com

Open Source Web Content Management Systems

Drupal	https://www.drupal.org
WordPress	https://wordpress.com

Customer Relationship Management Systems

Salesforce.com	http://www.salesforce.com
SugarCRM	http://sugarcrm.com
Infusionsoft	http://infusionsoft.com

Search Engine Marketing Resources

Google AdWords	https://www.google.com/adwords
Bing Ads	https://bingads.microsoft.com
SpyFu	http://spyfu.com
Moz Keyword Difficulty	https://moz.com/tools/keyword-difficulty
Wordtracker	http://wordtracker.com
Keyword Discovery	http://www.keyworddiscovery.com
Google Keyword Planner	https://adwords.google.com/Keyword-Planner
Web Robots Pages	http://www.robotstxt.org
XML Sitemaps Generator	http://www.xml-sitemaps.com
Moz Open Site Explorer	http://opensiteexplorer.org

Email Marketing Resources

Constant Contact	https://www.constantcontact.com
MailChimp	http://www.mailchimp.com
ExactTarget	http://www.exacttarget.com

Social Media Marketing Resources

Linkedin	https://www.linkedin.com
Twitter	https://twitter.com
Facebook	https://www.facebook.com
Google+	https://plus.google.com
YouTube	http://youtube.com
Vimeo	http://vimeo.com
Dailymotion	http://dailymotion.com
Metacafe	http://metacafe.com
SlideShare	http://slideshare.net
SlideCorner	http://slidecorner.com
SlideServe	http://slideserve.com
Pinterest	http://pinterest.com
Flickr	http://flickr.com
Picasa	http://picasa.google.com
Scribd	http://scribd.com
Issuu	http://issuu.com
Calameo	http://calameo.com

Mobile Marketing Resources

DudaMobile	http://www.dudamobile.com
Kaywa	http://kaywa.com
QR Stuff	http://qrstuff.com
ScanLife	http://scanlife.com

Analytics & ROI Measurement Resources

Google Analytics	https://www.google.com/analytics
Radian6 from Salesforce	http://salesforcemarketingcloud.com
Bitly	http://bit.ly

Resources

About the Author

Bob DeStefano is a B2B online marketing strategist and professional speaker with more than 20 years of experience helping distributors and manufacturers leverage online marketing to produce bottom-line results.

Through his speaking, writing and consulting, Bob makes online marketing understandable and empowers business leaders with actionable tips and strategies. Business leaders can use these strategies immediately to generate leads and sales, to strengthen relationships with customers, and to measure the return on marketing investments.

Bob earned an MBA from New York University, Stern School of Business, and a B.S. from Villanova University. His online marketing career began as a strategic planner for Dean Witter, Discover & Co. specializing in Internet and online marketing strategies. While at Dean Witter, Bob spearheaded the creation of the company's first website.

As founder and president of SVM E-Marketing Solutions, a leading B2B online marketing agency, Bob works with a wide variety of companies — from Fortune 500 companies to small family-owned businesses — to help them leverage online marketing to achieve bottom-line results.

Additionally, Bob serves as the endorsed online marketing consultant for a variety of industrial trade associations. Bob also contributes regularly to a variety of publications, including Modern Distribution Management and MarketingProfs, on the subject of actionable online marketing strategies. A member of the National Speakers Association, Bob has presented at many prestigious associations and companies.

Bob will use his online marketing expertise to ensure your company's online marketing strategies produce bottom-line results!

Hire Bob to Speak at your Next Event or Conference

Bob DeStefano is available for keynote presentations, educational workshops and full-day seminars. He is a frequent speaker at association conferences, trade shows and corporate events nationwide.

As an added bonus, after learning how to put online marketing to work, attendees can spend some one-on-one time with Bob to get an expert's opinion on how to turn their website into a money-maker. Bob can prepare a custom 40-page Online Marketing Analysis that will tell each attendee how to transform their website into their most powerful marketing tool.

Visit www.BobDeStefano.com for more information

or call (877) 786-3249 x3

About Gale Media, Inc.

Gale Media is a market-leading information services and publishing company. Its two business units – Modern Distribution Management and MDM Analytics (formerly Industrial Market Information) – provide knowledge products and services to professionals in industrial product and wholesale distribution markets.

Since 1967, MDM has been the definitive resource for distribution management best practices, competitive intelligence and market trends through its twice-monthly newsletter, market intelligence reports, books and conferences.

MDM Analytics provides proprietary market research and analytic services to profile market share and account potential for industrial products.

For more information, visit www.mdm.com.